CLIP CULTURE MANUAL

CLIP CULTURE MANUAL

Must-have business tips to increase clientele, grow profitably, and achieve the ultimate success

DAVID MICHAEL BROWN, MA

Licensed Master Barber and Entrepreneur

This publication is designed to provide competent and reliable information regarding the subject matter covered.

Copyright © 2021 by David Michael Brown.

ALL RIGHTS RESERVED WORLDWIDE

All rights reserved. In accordance with the U.S. Copyright Act of 1976, the scanning, uploading, and electronic sharing of any part of this book without the permission of the publisher is unlawful piracy and theft of the author's intellectual property. If you would like to use material from the book (other than for review purposes), prior written permission must be obtained by contacting the author at info@clipculturebarbershop.com.

Mynd Matters Publishing
715 Peachtree Street NE
Suites 100 & 200
Atlanta, GA 30308

ISBN: 978-1-953307-48-4 (pbk)
ISBN: 978-1-953307-49-1 (hdcv)
ISBN: 978-1-953307-50-7 (ebook)

Printed in the United States

To my best friend, the late Hugh Lee Boykin, Jr. aka HB, my mother Sharon Williams, my grandmother Elizabeth Young, my sister Olivia Brown, and my brother Nathaniel Brown.

CONTENTS

Introduction 13
Starting A Business In Tough. Keeping A Business Is Tougher ... 15
Rule #1: Eliminate All Unnecessary Cost 17
Brand Awareness 18
Introductions + Professionalism 19
Build A Demand 20
Pricing 21
Put Ego Aside 23
How Bad Do You Want It? 23
Invest In Your Craft, Artist And Vision Development 24
Fear And Perseverance 25
Social Media Presence 27
Adapt And Overcome 27
Uplift, Respect, Ambition, And Hustle 28
Energy 29
Set Goals 29
Discipline 31
Emotion Has Nothing To Do With Business. 31
Network 33
Network With Yourself 33
Dream Rich 34
Don't Expect More Than You Bring To The Table 37
Worth The Money 38
Business Reputation 39

Google Reviews 40
Consistency Brings More Money 41
What's Your Impact? 42
Be On Time 42
Power To Create 44
Break The Law As Far As What You Expect Out Of A Barber 45
Sanitation 47
Customer Service 48
Build A Base 49
Marketing Strategy 51
Grind State/Mind State 52
Work The Bottom Before Trying To Be At The Top 53
Skill Vs. Will 56
Morning Rush 57
Outside Noise + Distractions 59
Location, Location, Location 60
Booth Rent Vs. Commission 61
Cutting Hair Is My Talent, But Business Is My Passion 62
Your Clients Aren't Yo Homeboys 63
Customer Retention 66
Don't Worry About What The Next Is Doing 67
Working Works 69
Hot Money Attitude 70
Get Off Yo Phone 72
Social Media Branding 73
Trademark Your Brand 74

- Get A Business Account 76
- Brand Vs. Unbranded 77
- Respect The Business 78
- S.A.L.E. = Start The Sale. Ask Questions. Lead People To Buy. End The Sale 81
- Burning Out 82
- Lead Generation Calls 83
- Slow Motion Better Than No Motion 85
- Walk-In Flow 86
- Sweat Equity 87
- Business Cards 89
- Learn And Grow 91
- Rookies Should Outwork The Vets 92
- Quality Vs. Quantity 93
- Write It Down, Track Your Numbers 95
- Exit Strategy/Plan 96
- Structure 98
- Protect The Brand 98
- Taking A Leap 99
- Stop Falling For Every Social Media Gimmick 100
- A Wise Man Learns From His Mistakes. A Wiser Man Learns From Others' Mistakes 100
- Setup A Separate Way For Booth Renters To Pay You 101
- Collaborate Vs. Compete 102
- Be About Your Community 103
- What's Your Motivation? 104

Good Vides Only 105
Create Your Own Content 107
Know Your Audience 108
Ethics…Get Some 109
Capitalizing 110
Culture 112
What's Your Portfolio/Profile 112
Feedback 114
First Impressions 114
Freelance Or Free Loader? 116
Put Yo Name And Number In Everybody Phone 116
Face To Face Marketing 117
Direct Approach 119
Empathic Listening 120
How To Respond Gracefully 122
Even When You Lose The Passion, You Still Got To Work 123
Finance Before Romance 125
Don't Think About A Storefont Until You Have An Overflow. 127
People Buy Into You When They Know Your Story 129
Be Grateful For Every Client 130
A Title Does Not Make You A Leader 132
Don't Block Every Client 133
Give Your Clients A Proper Consult 135
Don't Do The Most To Get The Most 136
It Takes Money To Make Money 138
Don't Chase The Celebrity 138

Shop Talk: Ethics	140
Can't Teach Effort	141
Master One Thing First	143
Increase Your Value	144
The Root, The Start, The Beginning	146
Unplug	148
Photography	149
Career Visioning	150
Money Talks	152
Partnership Vs. Sole Proprietorship	153
Never Give Another Business Person All Your Money Until The Project Is Done	156
Keep Going!!!	157
Stay Away From Negative-Minded People	158
Your Business Ein	159
Bookkeeping	162
Purpose-Driven	162
Support Your Own	165
Take Emotions Out Of Business Decisions	165
Practical Tasks + Tips	167

INTRODUCTION

The Barber Industry is the second oldest profession in the world and the fastest growing in the United States. Given the massive growth and opportunity, everybody wants to get a piece of this industry. There are various reasons why people get into the barber/hair beauty industry. Some have a passion for the craft and some just want the money. Currently, the industry includes more than 80,000 establishments (77,000 beauty salons; 4,500 barber shops) with combined annual revenue of about $20B. With all the growth in the industry, right now is the perfect time to capitalize on what it has to offer. Barbers are the new rock stars. They are neighborhood heroes. People love their barber. The industry is wide open. With social media backing it, you can literally be as big and as "present" as you want to be.

Clip Culture Manual is designed to not only help barbers build their clientele, but to guide everyone in the health, wellness, and beauty industry to elevate and excel. The informative content provided from cover to cover will benefit stylists, makeup artists, fitness trainers, tattoo artists, nail techs, braiders, chefs, and a multitude of other professions.

Use this guide to test your drive, growth level, success factors, and character.

Welcome to the *Clip Culture Manual*. I hope you learn something new by taking this journey. This manual will test your drive, openness, integrity, and business acumen. At the end, you will know what you're doing right and what you need to work on. So, grab your notebook and popcorn and let's learn!

STARTING A BUSINESS IN TOUGH. KEEPING A BUSINESS IS TOUGHER.

Starting a business is one of the toughest things you can do in life. It's tough because it takes a lot of time and responsibility. The easiest thing to do is to work at your place of business and keep it moving. Starting a business is tough because you have to have all of your resources lined up for the business to thrive. Sometimes, you will be learning on the fly, which is fine. However, you want to be as prepared as possible. To start a business, you need a few things:

1. A substantial amount of clients
2. A contractor to (affordably) customize your establishment
3. A budget
4. A nest of money put aside in case the business doesn't pop right away
5. An engineer to design your floor plans
6. An interior designer who can bring your vision to life
7. Bomb ass location with good walk-in traffic
8. A graphic designer and printer to make your flyers, shirts, business cards, etc.

Having these eight things will help tremendously. Most importantly, you need the key people to help make the vision work. They are pivotal for a small business. Finding the right team is extremely tough. Basically, it's not their business or vision so you have to accept that they may not care as much.

You're fortunate when you find someone that does treat your business similar to how you treat your business.

Once you have everything in place, maintain your business can be even tougher because you have to change with the times and maintain a standard at the same time. Sometimes the people who work there become stagnant and unmotivated. When that happens, it's your job to make some strategic calls.

RULE #1: ELIMINATE ALL UNNECESSARY COST

As a business owner, you must understand the impact of unnecessary costs on your business. The more you can do to remove unneeded overhead, the better off you will be. Once you learn, you earn. Extremely high overhead can kill your business. Make a list of things you need, what are "nice-to-haves," and what you can do yourself to save money. Avoid being overcharged for a product or service that you can get for less. It starts with making an investment in your own materials and supplies. Read up on how to make things yourself. If your routine supplier's prices are too high, it will impact your prices and customer mix. Also limit simply buying the shiny objects that look good or make you feel successful but take from the bottom line instead of add to it. Try to find the best options for your business and eliminate anything that does not add to the bottom line.

BRAND AWARENESS

Brand Awareness is key. Most business owners, especially of new establishments, will not have the resources to plaster their name on every piece of advertising media in the market. Plus, increased exposure doesn't guarantee brand linkage or purchases. For heightened awareness of your brand, do the following:

1. Be visible within your community; consider sponsoring a relevant event
2. Be consistent in how your brand shows up across all social media profiles
3. Develop a hashtag strategy
4. Post regularly on all platforms
5. In person and on your personal profiles, aim to appropriately represent the establishment in which you work
6. Make it easy to gain and maintain new customers

Customers should not have to work overtime to find you or wonder about your hours of availability. Make it easy for them to find, pay, and refer you. One success tip is to make your business synonymous with the category or type of service/project. For example, when someone says, "I need a Kleenex®," they are referring to tissue in general while using a specific brand to identify the product. We know there are several tissue brands, however, Kleenex has created such a powerful industry presence, it is the household name in the category. Similar examples can be found with Band-Aid® (bandages).

INTRODUCTIONS + PROFESSIONALISM

Be a person and not a company. As the owner, every customer needs to know your name. Introduce yourself in a professional manner. For example, you can say, "Hi, my name is John Doe." People like to know the person behind the brand. Your clients want to connect with you, therefore, give the behind-the-scenes every now and then to help people connect you to your brand. Be open to tell your story everywhere you go to deepen the customer connection and relationship. People spend money with people they know and feel comfortable with being around.

Once the person becomes a regular client, never compromise on professionalism. As an entrepreneur, you want to keep respect in your business. With that being said, you must watch what you say—keep everything business. Never get too relaxed with your clients because regardless of how casual it feels, it is about business first and foremost. Every client is NOT your friend. Greet them with care. Give them handshakes. Look every client in the eyes. Engage with them fully. Keep yourself neat at all times. You have to look the part of the service you are providing.

BUILD A DEMAND

Get your skills up! You have to be one of the best in your profession. Become a student of the industry. Follow the trends in the market. Also, don't be afraid to create your own trend. Master your craft. When you have free time, sit with someone in the shop whose skills you admire and learn from them. Add different techniques to your skillset. Clients are going to notice and appreciate it. Developing and mastering your skills can take years and countless hours of practice.

PRICING

In today's market, everyone wants to charge high prices without putting in the work for it. I believe you have to be in demand first before you take your prices up no matter if you feel as though you have a higher skillset than others. For example, charging $40 out the gate to potential new clients may rub them the wrong way. You have to be talented at $20 before you start charging more. Clients can also feel when you just want the money. Energy doesn't lie. People want to feel good about who they are giving their hard-earned dollars to. Remain competitive in the market and never forget the goal—longevity. Not a quick dollar.

There's a difference between competitive and premium. Competitive means the average price in the market is a particular number and you stay within the $5 to $10 range. Premium is when your prices are higher than the average. This limits the number of people who will consider your services. Being competitive will give you a better quantity of clientele. Every entrepreneur is entitled to set their own prices. However, when you go premium, it needs to be worth it because customers will know if they are getting a premium service.

PUT EGO ASIDE

Sometimes you're going to have to swallow your pride to get ahead. Never think you are better than the people you serve. Some barbers/stylists treat their clients who have been patronizing them for years like they don't even matter. Don't serve yourself, serve the people. Yes, your talent can be an amazing attribute. But how you treat the people is what matters most. Check your attitude at the door. Nobody wants to give money to an arrogant prick.

HOW BAD DO YOU WANT IT?

What drives you to be an entrepreneur? Is it the money? Is it notoriety? Or, do you like to make the people feel good? Everyone is entitled to their own opinion. But going the extra mile is key. That's what determines greatness.

Do you wake up thinking about how great you can be? Chasing greatness is what separates you from average or mediocre. The attention is in the details. Always check your work to see if you're progressing. Take pictures of your work and compare them to newer work. If you're not progressing, you're regressing. Clients know when your skills haven't improved over the years. Remain a student of the game. Remain teachable. You're only going to get better if you want it. Each day, ask yourself if you've gotten better. Ask others to critique your work, too. Feedback is essential to your progression.

INVEST IN YOUR CRAFT, ARTIST AND VISION DEVELOPMENT

If you want to be one of the best, you have to invest in your craft. You have to buy the tools that will help you perform better. Try different tools and compare each tool. Different tools do different things. Also, invest in your appearance. Barbers/Stylists attract people that look like them. Be presentable. A custom cape or apron would be nice. Buy the best tools. Look your best and give your best. These things will ensure you will have clients for a long time to come. It's not fair or professional to borrow your co-worker's equipment and tools. If you are working and making money, buy what you need.

Focus on personal growth. To standout in this industry, you have to tap into your artistic side, which means you have to be open to doing promotional videos, going to hair shows, participating in hair shows, looking the part, and investing in professional photos. Whatever it is that helps you as an artist, tap into your zone and go for it. Some clients don't mind when you do something creative with their hair. Being a barber/stylist is about being bold, being fierce, and trying new things. Bring the flava and be the flava. Being creative starts from within. The best artists normally display their artistic side in everything they do. Do not limit yourself.

Vision is something you need in several spectrums. In order to complete a good to great service, you must first visualize the process from start to finish. After you visualize what you have to do, then you put it into action. Execution is key. Barbers/Stylists should also listen to what the client or customer is requesting and try to provide the best service based on their ability. It is okay to make suggestions about what you may think looks or works best. You are the artist and are responsible for bringing that creation to life. What you visualize always carries out in your work.

FEAR AND PERSEVERANCE

Let go of fear. You can't operate in it. Fear is the illusion of something that doesn't exist. If you're going to be in this industry, you cannot be afraid to take risks. That's a part of being an entrepreneur and artist. You have to continue to push yourself to greatness. You cannot be afraid to let people go and you can't be afraid to try new things. Don't let fear and doubt determine what you do for yourself. Many people allow fear to stop them from ever getting started. You never know what you can be, if you allow fear to become a barrier in your goals. We are all hesitant about some things. However, we have to be willing to take a chance on ourselves.

Be able to prevail. Sometimes things won't go the way you want but it is critical to stay the course. Clients may leave, walk-ins may slowdown but whatever comes your way, keep going.

SOCIAL MEDIA PRESENCE

Social media is what's driving the hair industry. Your social media presence is vital to your success. In today's market, social media is an extension of your resume. Old clients and even potential clients, can tell right away whether you're serious about business or not. Your social media platform should be about you and what you do. This is how you capture an audience. When posting, be sure to have the right lighting, best quality camera, and find an ideal angle. All of these things are integral in your presentation.

Post your work consistently. Show variety. People love to see when you can do multiple services. Use hashtags under your post. This helps you get more exposure. Your posts should attract and influence people from many miles away. Monitor your content. Stay away from too many things that have nothing to do with how you get paid on your social media page. Likes on Instagram don't always turn into dollars. Barbers/Stylists still need to hustle. Social media is great but it is still all about the interaction between barber and client.

ADAPT AND OVERCOME

Adapt to your surroundings in your industry. You may not always be working in the best condition but you have to do the best you can. Create the atmosphere and environment you want for you and your clients. Set the tone in your work station. Make your clients feel as though they are safe in any environment that you bring to them. If you don't adapt and overcome, the time will pass you by. The game is always changing and evolving. Move with the times. It's in your benefit. You don't have to recreate the wheel, you just have to keep the ball rolling.

UPLIFT, RESPECT, AMBITION, AND HUSTLE

Uplift your clients, co-workers, and businesses around you. This is a brotherhood. Learn as much as you can and help others as much as you can. You can't put a price on ambition. It comes from within. You have to get out in the marketplace and get it. Nothing good comes to those who sit around and wait.

Respect thy neighbor. Respect your co-workers. Respect the barber industry. Operate with integrity. Respect goes a long way in this industry. Hustle the long way. Pass out a million flyers. Promote yourself and your business as much as you can. Get out and talk to people. Build up a buzz for yourself.

ENERGY

The energy you put out is the energy you're going to get back. If you put out good energy, you will get back good energy. If you put out bad energy, you will get back bad energy. Think positive at all times. As long as you're going forward, that's what matters. Bad energy messes up the money. People can feel tension or bad energy in the room. People can also feel good energy. People know when someone cares and when someone doesn't. Keep a smile on your face. Say a prayer in the morning before you start your day. Drink plenty of water. Keep the attitude and the mindset that your goal is to serve paying customers that want and need what you do.

SET GOALS

Goals should be broken down into short-term and long-term goals. Goals will keep you on track. If you don't have goals, then you're just existing. Ask yourself where you want to be in three to five years. Then ask yourself where you want to be five to ten years. Next, you have to apply it to what you are doing. There should be a quota set up for what you want to reach each day.

DISCIPLINE

Discipline is the practice of training people to obey rules or a code of behavior, using punishment to correct disobedience. Discipline is more valuable than motivation. Some people confuse discipline for motivation. However, it's two different things. Motivation will get you to start something, but discipline will determine the result of what you start. Things are always going to happen. There may be a few things that can get you off track. However, when you have a foundation of discipline, you can succeed. You have to train yourself to do things on repeat that will help you reach your goals. If you don't have discipline, you will never reach your maximum potential. Eliminate any distractions and push forward.

EMOTION HAS NOTHING TO DO WITH BUSINESS.

Get out of your feelings and get this money. Now, I understand all money isn't good money. Some clients are annoying and bring unnecessary hassle. However, whenever you are in an entrepreneurial field, you're playing the numbers game. Your job is to produce volume. How many clients can you see in a day? You must have the desire to do this. You cannot operate with the mindset of, *Let me get three or four people then I'm going home.* That doesn't help you.

You have to operate as a go-getter. Someone who is hungry for success. Being a go-getter does not mean you have to be cutthroat. Schedule your clients the right way and always look for more. If there's a client who gets on your nerve, talk to them about it before you cut them off. Or, pass them along to another independent contractor in your establishment so the money can remain in the business. Customer retention is key and has to be taken seriously for any business to survive.

NETWORK

Network with everyone you meet. You never know where that connection will take you. Normally, everyone has a gift, talent, or skill that can help them grow. One's network determines their net worth. Life is all about having resources and options. There is nothing wrong with attacking your goals alone. That's what you supposed to do.

However, if you are looking to grow, you're going to need a bit of help at some point. None of us know it all. Building a clientele with an array of talents and gifts are a beautiful thing. So many people have to seek out information or pay to get time from certain individuals. However, when the information is coming to you, you get a lot of information firsthand without having to pay for it. Now that's play talk.

NETWORK WITH YOURSELF

Go get it for yourself. Build yo shit up. Don't go out chasing celebrities for clout. Work so hard until the people you couldn't reach, reach out to you. Celebrities don't respect you when you chase after them. Instead, treat your regular, everyday clients like celebrities.

There's nothing wrong with networking, but don't be a dick rider. There's a difference. Don't be arrogant, but be confident in your abilities. Be confident in who you are and what you bring to the table. When you know your worth, you don't have to chase anyone. When your resume is strong, your clients will refer new clients to you. If you are putting out good work and your energy is good, people will come. You attract people just like you. So, if you're a good person and have talent, the opportunities are limitless. Be your own biggest cheerleader. Nobody can support you more than you.

DREAM RICH

No matter where you start, you can finish at the top. You may have been born poor, but if you dream rich, you can be successful and accomplish anything. Dreams do come true. However, they come true with hard work and dedication. If your dreams aren't big enough to the point that they scare you, you're not dreaming big enough.

Your dreams are yours. Nobody can take them from you. These are your thoughts, visions, and emotions. When you dream rich, you are now dreaming of changing your circumstances and possibly your family's circumstances, as well. Dreaming Rich is simply doing the things that could change your family structure a few generations over. Dreaming Rich is gaining financial freedom so you can be able to do the necessities for yourself. Also, when you Dream Rich, you give back. You are able to pour into others. You can share your thoughts and experiences with others on how you go where you are today.

YOU HAVE TO HAVE **FAITH** TO MAKE IT. WHAT YOU BELIEVE IN WILL MANIFEST ITSELF **ON ITS OWN.** CONTINUE TO WORK YOUR PLAN; BUT **ALWAYS BELIEVE IN YOURSELF AND THE TALENT** GOD GAVE YOU.

DON'T EXPECT MORE THAN YOU BRING TO THE TABLE

This topic is broad and can apply it to a lot of things. Barbers always complain about the shop being slow. Barbers complain about not enough walk-ins or walk-in traffic in general. Now, some locations are not in the best area. However, that's why you should do your research before you commit to a location. In the meantime, look at what you as a barber bring to the establishment. Do you have clients? Are you a powerhouse salesperson that can effectively bring people in? The shop is only responsible for so much marketing and walk-in traffic. If you're coming in with nothing and doing nothing to create that traffic for yourself, you have no right to complain.

With the right marketing strategy, you can be busy at any location. So many times, barbers sit on their phone and don't do anything! The only time they get up is to charge their phone and scroll up and down on social media. If you don't have a minimum of $1,000 worth of weekly clients on your phone, you should be getting out there to build it up.

Stop depending on the shop for everything. Barbers claim to be independent contractors, but all of their actions are dependent of the shop flow. If you are going to operate with the mindset of being dependent on the shop, then you should be on commission not booth rent because you're not putting anything in. You get back what you put out in this industry. It's grind over shine. Sometimes you have to work countless hours to get where you are going. Don't be afraid to commit to the grind. It will be worth it in the end.

WORTH THE MONEY

Your service has to match the price. Can you drive a demand for yourself? Can you keep clientele? Are people willing to drive more than thirty minutes to see you? Do you deliver every time you step in the booth? These are questions you have to ask yourself and make a real assessment as to where you are in the industry.

There are a lot of factors that go into whether you're worth the money or not. People work hard to earn their income. Clients want to feel good about who they are giving their money to. Clients will be loyal to you and come very often if you're worth the money. Clients will also pay the listed prices without complaint if you provide a level of service equivalent to what they expect.

BUSINESS REPUTATION

Too many times, barbers/stylists don't care about the reputation and integrity of the business. However, how you treat the business reflects the brand, the reputation, etc. Barbers should really consider how they treat a business as it directly affects your money.

If you have an I-don't-give-a-shit attitude, that could potentially mess up money for everyone in the business. The owner shouldn't be the only person to protect the shield of the business. Every person who works in the establishment should handle it with care. No one expects for things to be perfect, but if one person is always causing an issue and not producing, that person doesn't deserve to be there. The goal is for people to come back and refer as many people as possible. It's pivotal for clients and future clients to be used to a standard of greatness. The business's core values, integrity, goals and reputation should never be jeopardized due to a lack of professionalism, class, or understanding

Though some barbers may work as independent contractors, it speaks volumes when you try to ensure the business as a reputable one. It's easy to find fault in previous establishments, but are people asking themselves, "What can I do to make things better?"

...instead of shop hopping?

What clients and walk-ins see and feel each time they visit an establishment, determines a shop's reputation. Perception outside looking in can sometimes make or break you. Your shot can be A-1 but all it takes is for a few clients to say:

1. They were loud using profanity
2. They were sleeping in the chairs
3. The barbers didn't look well-groomed

GOOGLE REVIEWS

A new client could be just a click away. If you're in business, your Google reviews are crucial. One way to build it up is to ask all of your clients to give you a five-star review. The five-star review means everything. Get as many of those as you can. Potential clients are always checking reviews. People want to know what level of service they are getting before they enter your establishment. Reviews really matter. It helps your business grow tremendously. Everything is on Google and your business should be as well. This is free advertisement for your business. Ratings can make or break your business. Too many bad reviews can hurt your business.

CONSISTENCY BRINGS MORE MONEY

Consistency brings steady clients. It's hard for some barbers to stay consistent. The more consistent you are the more money you will make. However, when you are all over the place, your money will be funny. To maximize on your potential, it's best you set a goal and routine for yourself. Consistency is the key to longevity, stability, and growth. Those are the things you need to survive in business.

WHAT'S YOUR IMPACT?

When you're done being a barber/stylist, how do you want to be remembered? If you aren't a barber/stylist, how do you want to be remembered? Were you innovative? Were you creative? Were you there for the people when they needed you? Being a barber is bigger than just cutting hair. You're so much more to people. Sometimes you're a brother, friend, counselor, mentor, etc.

Coming to the shop and seeing a familiar face bring so much joy for some. Some barbers have the luxury of seeing kids grow into adults, and they still come to them. When brothers, uncles, sons, mothers can bring their children and family members to you for years, that's amazing. That's bigger than what money can do for you. The relationships you are building are rich.

BE ON TIME

Be on time. Simple as that. The days of people sitting in the barbershop for hours are over. People want convenience. Nobody wants to sit around for two hours to get a haircut. It doesn't matter how good you are or think you are. Being on time is a sign of respect. In the meantime, things happen and things do come up. However, you should NOT be hours behind every time. Being continually late is a sign of disrespect and a sure way to lose clients. If you struggle with being on time for your clients, there are user-friendly booking apps available to help you. Clients absolutely love booking apps. It helps cut down on waiting on text message appointment questions. Using the booking system also allows the barbers/stylists to be more organized. It gives the clients options and times that fit their schedule. All the barber has to do is be present.

As stated before, availability is the best ability. When you're constantly late, clients tend to complain to the other barbers in the shop about your tardiness. If the tardiness continues, clients will eventually go to other barbers in the shop. The barber game will give you enough rope to hang yourself. Some will never come back if you're routinely late and unfortunately, bad news travels faster than good news. Lateness effects the reputation of the business. Constantly being late normally tells a lot about you as a person. Talent alone doesn't always keep people but consistency will. Just because you're an independent contractor, doesn't mean you should abuse other people's schedule. Come to work. Do what you need to do, and go home.

POWER TO CREATE

The power to create is a special thing. Most barbers have a creative side. The lines, designs, blends, sharpness are all a part of it. Barbers who are really in tune with their craft make hair contact before they make eye contact. Barbers who like to create and be artist look for clients who they can transform. Barbers who just want money only look for clients to make money off.

When you're passionate about your craft, the way you feel about your work shows. Every client is a new canvas to work on. It's a fresh start. Cutting hair is a form of fashion and a way to express yourself. Barbers are artists. Tunisonal artist to be exact. There are always new funky styles that people are willing to try. You just have to find the people who will allow you to create. High school and college students normally let you try new things with their hair. Being bold, being innovative, and being a trendsetter set you apart in this business.

In your free time, consider sketching different hairstyles. Also, screenshot other people's work and recommend it to your clients. The only way you're going to get better at it is to try it out. Sports athletes, rappers, and other entertainers love being able to say they got the flyest cut somewhere. Rappers like Nas and singers like Bobby Brown had signature haircuts. When you're able to create a signature style like Odell Beckham's haircut, you become legendary.

BREAK THE LAW AS FAR AS WHAT YOU EXPECT OUT OF A BARBER

It's sad to say but there's a good many people who don't expect much out of a barber. The perception is based on previous experiences with different barbers. As barbers and stylists, we can help change that narrative by how we interact with our clients.

In the meantime, we can't help it if someone looks down on our profession. Some people perceive barbers as flunky's who had to turn to barbering because of a sketchy past. That's not always the case. There are many barbers/stylists who carry themselves as professionals and business people. Your conversation and who you are as a person will dictate all of that. Clients love engaging with an intelligent, knowledgeable, and articulate person. No one wants a loud and rowdy person over their head talking about nothing. Bad conversation and energy mess up the money.

When you're with your clients, engage with them. Tell them a bit about yourself. Gain their trust. When you do the little things and separate yourself from the rest, it shows. Be a business person who is a barber. Expand your business. Have t-shirts and products on hand to sell. When clients see you have a variety of services, they began to take your seriously. Clients can get basic services anywhere. There's nothing wrong with basic services, but if you want to change the narrative, give clients something they cannot get anywhere else. You can be inclusive and exclusive at the same time.

SANITATION

Keep your work station and area clean. Nobody wants to come to a dirty space for a haircut. A dirty un-sanitized area will run a lot of people away. Germs and bacteria are real. People pay attention to the first thing they see. To keep your area clean does not take a lot of work. It just requires attention and care. If you don't care how your work station looks, that says a lot about you. Dirty clippers are a client's worst nightmare. Nobody wants to catch a ring worm due to unsanitized clippers. In between every cut, brush off your blades, oil your clippers, and reorganize your station. Keep your work area neat and clean.

Cleanliness should always be at the top of your agenda. That's the first thing people see when they walk into the shop. All outside/inside mirrors should be clean at all times. When you're done with your client, clean your space right away. Don't leave hair and neck stripes everywhere then walk off. That makes the business look bad. You always have to think about what the people coming in will think. Most people aren't comfortable with junk and clutter. Some people will decide who they want cutting their hair based on cleanliness alone. Presentation is everything. Don't let your trash can overflow with garbage. Wipe down your station and chair at night before you go home. Letting dirt build around your clippers and station until the next day is not cool. Dispose of all dirty razors. Dirty razors should be placed in the proper container. Hands should be washed and sanitized after every service.

CUSTOMER SERVICE

Great customer service is pivotal to any business's success. The level of customer service determines whether people come back or not. The level of customer services determines whether clients will recommend others to your business. Sometimes you don't have to have the greatest product if your customer service is on point.

Great customer service includes greeting customers at the door, saying thank you after each service, and getting to each person in a timely manner. If you can do these things, you will be assured to have plenty of clients and business. Bad customer service includes being late, being rude to customers, not speaking to customers when they arrive, and coming to work smelling like weed or alcohol.

One of the problems with independent contractors is them feeling like they don't have to give great customer service because they work for themselves. That's a big mistake and the wrong attitude. We are in the service industry and are here to serve. Some independent contractors have lost touch or may have never trained on the *service* element. Some independent contractors treat their clients like they are doing them a favor. This thinking means you're serving yourself, not the client. You have to keep an attitude of gratitude in order to prosper. No one person or company has ever reached the top of their industry with poor customer service. It doesn't cost you anything to be curious, kind, and treat people with respect. Great customer service helps separate your brand or your business from others.

BUILD A BASE

Before you open up a business, you definitely have to build a base. If you build up a real customer base, people will follow you. When you're first starting in the industry, you're a rookie. When you are new, you have to accept as many clients as you can. You need everyone from eight to eighty years-old. Basically, you are focusing on volume.

A great way to start is to market yourself to kids. Kids always need cuts and most experienced barbers don't want to do it. Cutting kids are a good filler until you can cut more teens and adults. The parents will eventually give you a chance to cut them as well—once they are comfortable with you. Building a base is about the ground work. This means you have to get out and market yourself. Mass grocery stores, gas stations, schools, car dealerships, etc. should be your target. Once you build you your clientele, you can decide what's your main niche.

Understand what age group of people come to see you most often. Knowing this can help you decide in which direction to go. The 22-50 age group is a good one to be in. People between those ages still care about looking good and will patronize the business more often.

The best time to build a base is Monday through Thursday. Those are the real grind days. Early week is perfect for going out and meeting people. During the early week, you get a chance to talk with clients and build a relationship. Friday through Sunday should just be extra. Monday through Thursday is the time to grind and network.

MARKETING STRATEGY

When you come to a new establishment, be sure you come with a marketing plan or overarching strategy. You should always know how you are going to market yourself. Don't rely on the door, walk-ins, referrals, or what you think the business can do for you. Come with a plan. Have flyers, business cards, and a business page ready.

Every area you work in will be different. Some areas need more marketing than others. YWhen you go to a new area, it is pivotal for you to pass out at least sixty flyers or cards each day for nine days. Only about 10% of those clients will come. However, you still want to put yourself out there. The biggest thing is creating a strong base. The more people that know you, the better. If you have been at an establishment for more than sixty days and you are still struggling to build clientele, something is wrong with your marketing strategy.

The number one question is whether you can get people in the door. Can you get people in the door the same day? Conversation rules the nation. Do you have what it takes to convince people that you can cut their hair the way they like it and be their regular barber? Going outside and holding a sign, marketing yourself, is a great way to build new clientele. Customers love when you interact with them, offer specials, or first cut, half off. Do things to get people to try you out for the first time.

GRIND STATE/MIND STATE

Grind state is all about how hard you are willing to go. How bad do you want it? Different things motivate people in different ways. When you are grinding—really grinding, you just want to get to the money. That's not a bad thing because when you're talented and passionate about your craft, you should be compensated. Someone in grind mode is focused. Grind state is someone on a mission to accomplish a goal. Basically, they are trying to get it. Someone who is on their grind gets up early in the morning and normally stays up late. When you are in that grind state, you are trying to get as many needs in as you can in one day. When you're in the zone like that, nothing or no one can stop you. Even when you're tired, the people you serve will give you the extra energy you need to get by. People who grind and people who hustle all recognize each other. All the hustlers acknowledge each other because they know what it takes to be successful. Everything we go through is mostly mental. Regardless of what you're going through, there are normally two options: 1) make progress or 2) make excuses. Remember you don't fix your problem, you fix your thinking. The problems will fix themselves. When your mind tells you that you can do anything, that's what you will do. It's grind over shine. You have to be a bit crazy and very relentless to go after your goals. When you are grinding, no one can stop you and nothing can stand in your way.

WORK THE BOTTOM BEFORE TRYING TO BE AT THE TOP

Be a good team member before trying to be the chief. A lot of people don't understand their roles or positions within a company. Everybody wants to be at the top without putting in the work or sacrifice to climb or build.

Being at the bottom of the totem pole is not demeaning or degrading. There is a lot of power in being at the bottom of the totem pole. The boss role isn't always glamorous as there is more responsibility placed on the boss/owner/shop manager. Focusing on the team is about going the extra mile for the business. A lot of people are afraid to go hard for the business because they either feel like they don't own it so it doesn't matter or they don't see what's in it for them and therefore don't care.

There is nothing is wrong with being a good team member. Come in, bust yo ass, get yo money, and go home. In the meantime, do the little things like take out the trash, sweep the floors, pass out flyers, wipe down the windows, promote the business, etc. without someone asking you to do it. Everyone notices hard work. Customers also notice who's doing what. Clients appreciate when they can validate your work ethic. When you become the boss or manager, you still have to set the example. Sometimes you gotta be the boss and the worker. Sometimes you have to still clean the restroom, be the janitor, do the marketing, fold the towels, wash the capes, etc. There's a lot that goes into it. Business ownership is not about instant gratification. Some want the title of being a boss, but not the work that comes with it. If you are not willing to do the extras to be a chief, stay put as a member of the team and play that role well.

SKILL VS. WILL

Either it's a skill or a will. If you have the will, the skill will come. You have to have the desire to be great. Often in this industry, few people have both. There are some with supreme talent and not hustle. There are some who are not as talented but hustle hard to make it. If there's a will, there's a way. Some barbers have to will their way through a particular cut because they don't have the natural talent. However, sometimes people will work with the individual that goes hard vs. the person who doesn't want to work at all. Many times, talented people don't want to feel obligated to work hard. However, the secret to success is working hard when no one is looking. Sometimes you have to make money even when you don't want to.

Talent will get you in the door. Work ethic will keep you in the door. Some of the most talented barbers/stylists have been the worst workers. These problems occur because these particular individuals don't have a goal in mind and don't want it to feel like a job. They want to come in when it's convenient, make some money, then go home. But that is not realistic. Well, not in the form of real success. Treating the business like a fast food order doesn't help you or the business at all. Operating is if you don't care impacts the reputation of the business tremendously. A skill is something you can acquire, but your will is internal. You have to believe you are a great barber. You have to get up every day with that in you in order for you to perform at a high level.

Passion + Hussle + Greatness + Skills are great but will only take you so far. You have to be in love with the grind for everything to manifest into something beautiful.

MORNING RUSH

So much happens in the morning but often, barbers neglect the morning rush. Once you start to think like a customer, you'll recognize the value of getting in and out earlier in the day, leaving plenty of time to handle everything else on the to-do list.

Depending on location and the foot traffic of your business, you could be missing out on a lot of new clients. There's an estimated three to five new customers coming into the business each week as first time walk-ins. The window of opportunity for these morning rush customers is between 9AM-11:30AM. These are the people who have meetings after lunch, have to work late, or simply have something to do in the afternoon. If barbers take advantage of the morning rush, there could potentially be fifteen to twenty new clients in their database. If you're just getting to work at noon or later, there is so much you've likely missed. The motive should always be to do as much as you can by 3PM. If you're hustling to the maximum, you can still go home before 5PM.

The morning rush is important because that's how you set the tone for your day. Get up with the mindset to go get it. In the morning, so many things are happening and moving around. Don't miss out on those sales because you get too wrapped up in the comfort of your bed. Getting a few walk-ins or going out to meet people is a good way to build your clientele. People will realize that you are reliable and will start booking with you regularly.

OUTSIDE NOISE + DISTRACTIONS

Can't let your personal problems spill over into the business. When you come to work, refocus your emotions and adjust your energy at the door. Your clients and co-workers shouldn't have to feel what you are going through in your personal life. It's understood that things happen. However, you have to be mentally strong enough to channel that energy and get through the day. Outside noise is real.

So many barbers are distracted by everything, but work. Everything besides work means more. It shouldn't be that way. It's understood you will have a life outside of work. However, work is how we eat. Work is how we survive. Working helps build character. Work defines who we are as a people. Issues with significant others, family, or friends do not put money in your pocket or help you focus. Having the ability to focus and be intentional is a major key to success. You got to be locked in to what you do to reach the full potential of talent you possess. Don't let things or people who can't help you take you away from your money. If you are an entrepreneur, minimize all distractions. When you step into work, it's time to perform. In order to be the best version of you, there can't be things that stop you from getting there. Cut anything that no longer benefits where you're trying to go.

LOCATION, LOCATION, LOCATION

Location plays a big role in the frequency and volume of shop flow. Now, location does not stop you from making money. It's up to each independent contractor to turn it up on their own. However, the shop does need to have some type of flow. When selecting a place to work, it is important to find an establishment with visibility and foot traffic. Shops located in strip plazas make it a bit tougher for barbers to attract new clients without foot traffic. The barber has to work twice as hard to get new people. However, it does not mean it can't be done.

In the meantime, a barbershop in a plaza with an anchor store with several other businesses in it is like striking gold. When your salon/barbershop is in a plaza with an anchor store such as Wal-Mart, Target, or Trader Joe's, that alone will generate traffic. Clients like being able to come to a location where they can get many things done. People like convenience and variety. Do your research on where you want to work. See what best fits you and your clients. Parking is a big deal. If clients can't park or get in and out with ease, that could also cause problems.

BOOTH RENT VS. COMMISSION

Booth rent is what most independent contractors prefer because it's more beneficial for them. However, commission is what most business owners prefer because booth rent gives the barbers too much control. Booth rent was set up for barbers and independent contractors to get their hustle on. The average booth rent is about $200. Once the barber/stylist makes their booth rent money, the rest of it is profit. If a barber was interested in having his/her own shop, this would be the quickest way to get established.

Most barbers don't want to pay commission because it would force them to work harder, pay taxes up front, and they would be official employees.

Most people who are willing to work on a commission-basis are straight out of school and need a fresh start. People with an established client list don't want to pay commission. A commission-based establishment can thrive, if the money made off commission is invested back into the business for marketing. Some barbers would work on commission if they knew the walk-in traffic was going to be high. Most commission-based shops are located in malls where first-timers and walk-ins will always be. Having a commission-based shop in a bad location is definitely not a good idea. The bad thing about booth rent is barbers leaving the business stuck with no warning. The shop then has to find new booth renters quickly to pay for the chairs. In commission establishments, the business collects money first. Commission is the best way to go if in the best location. Booth rent is okay but it's tough for a business to duplicate itself with unstable income. Commission-base shops last longer, if managed correctly.

CUTTING HAIR IS MY TALENT, BUT BUSINESS IS MY PASSION

Every independent contractor is not an entrepreneur. The entrepreneurial spirit isn't something you can buy. Either you have it or you don't. If you do have it, you will get out there and get it. When you want it badly, that's all you think about.

True entrepreneurs are always thinking about how they are going to get paid. There are thousands of ways to get paid and a true entrepreneur is going to figure it out. The average or below average independent contractor is going to do the bare minimum to get by. When you're an entrepreneur, you look for ways to evolve. It's not all about the money either. It's about the thrill of new opportunity and creating things that people love, want, and need. Doing new business deals are exciting. Financial freedom is the goal. To be in a position where you don't have to depend on one source of income is a great feeling. However, you have to master one source of income first before you start branching off into other endeavors. Once you have your main source of income secured, you can start looking into other options of entrepreneurship. Depending on the industry you're in, try to supply products and goods that coincide with what you already have in progress.

YOUR CLIENTS AREN'T YO HOMEBOYS

Take every client you have seriously. It's understood that you will make friends and relationships with clients. However, some lines should never be crossed. If you look at your client like a friend and not a client, you start treating them like a friend and not as though they are paying for a service or product. Always respect your client as a client. They are paying you for a service.

Don't tell your clients all of your business. Clients will leave and never come back over certain things you may have said. You will never be able to please everyone but try avoid giving people a reason not to come back. Bad press is a reflection on you and the business.

People respect that extra level of professionalism. Hanging out or doing outside business not related to how you regularly do business is not always a good thing either. If a business deal with your client goes sour, it can ruin a relationship. Your clients should respect you for the work you do not because you are cool to hang out with. Always keep it business. When you start hanging out with your clients too much, that's when they start asking for discounts or deals on your services. Friends like discounts. Don't create an uncomfortable situation for everyone involved.

THE DAY YOU PLANT THE SEED IS NOT THE DAY YOU EAT THE FRUIT

CUSTOMER RETENTION

So many times, barbers complain about walk-in traffic. They have barely any hustle and their favorite line is, "Man, that shop's slow." However, the question to ask is, "Is the shop slow or are you slow?"

If the shop provides you with fifteen walk-ins per week, it's your responsibility to get the other fifteen people per week to help you grow. In the meantime, if you have been at a particular establishment for more than three months and you are solely waiting on the door, then you have a customer retention problem. If you do the math, you will understand the dilemma. Approximately sixty new clients per month for three months is 180 people. Those 180 should be multiplying and it doesn't take long. If you are not retaining clients, something is wrong with your marketing strategy, pricing, skill level, customer service, time management, or all of these. Every three months, assess where you are and ask yourself a few important questions.

Is my business growing?

Do I understand what my customers think/feel about me and my business?

What can I work on to be better?

It's not right to point the finger and blame the business for your lack of progression. Hopping from shop to shop doesn't help either. You have to stay down until you come up. Truly, you can make any location busy. It's all about your work ethic and drive. It's important to take care of every client you have. Every opportunity you get is your chance to grow your business. However, if you treat someone like a number instead of a client, they will feel that and not come back. In the meantime, if you treat someone like a client and give them the ultimate experience, they will return. It's all about your approach.

DON'T WORRY ABOUT WHAT THE NEXT IS DOING

Stay in your own lane and don't worry about what the next barber is doing. Plus, there's less traffic when you stay in your own lane. Don't get caught up in what others are doing. Following them will have you unconsciously picking up their bad habits and going in the wrong direction.

When you are doing what you need to do, the universe will bless you in ways you could not imagine. Don't worry about who is using enhancements on a cut. Don't worry about another person's barbering skills. Don't worry about how may clients you have versus what the next person has. Just worry about bettering yourself, perfecting your craft, and paying your booth rent on time.

Barbers sometimes focus on the wrong things. There are enough clients for everybody. If what the next person is doing is not going to benefit you, there's nothing to talk about. Independent contractors tend to think what works for them should work for everybody. That's not true. There's a client out there for every kind of business. Find your niche. Create your own and stay there. Nobody's opinion is law. At the end of the day, we are all at work to make money, not be concerned with what the next person does. If someone is not holding their own or not doing what they are supposed to do, it will show. Father time tells no lie. While at work all emphasis should be put on the work you are doing and nothing else.

WORKING WORKS

The quickest way to be successful is to work. There is no magic dust. If you want to have longevity, you have to work. Working works.

May times, independent contractors do not want the pressure of being on a schedule. However, you have to set a routine for yourself. You have to know you're going to show up for work and stay a minimum of eight hours whether you have clients or not. The people who are normally super successful did not always know how they would make it but they never gave up. Giving up should never be an option. You may have to change up sometimes but never give up. Whatever it is you start, you need to finish.

Working builds character. Working gives you structure. Working provides your every need. Working is how we survive. Anything worth having, you have to work for it. If you don't work, you don't eat. It's really just that simple. It's called putting in your time. No real growth can happen in your business or personal life if you don't work at it. We all get tired and drained at times. However, sometimes, you have to kick in that extra gear to get to the next level.

Working works. Most business owners, CEOs, etc. had to work hard and grind prior to getting where they are today. Always put in your time. Your work will speak for itself. Clients know the people who are serious about their craft. A person who likes what they do for a living normally doesn't consider what they are doing as work. However, you still have to be there when you are running a business.

HOT MONEY ATTITUDE

The hot money attitude is someone who is looking to make about $150-$200 max per day then leave the business hanging and go about their day. A person with the hot money attitude is really ruining the business. Normally, the individual with the hot money attitude has no intention of staying more than four to five hours max. Most people with this mindset don't have a large client list because of a lack of skills, will, and disciple.

Individuals with the hot money attitude normally express themselves by saying things such as, "I'm just trying to get this money real quick." This type of person preys on walk-ins. They will do the service, get the money, and won't give out their contact information. They have no intention of building a relationship with clients. This type of mindset is not good for the business because when customers return and they look for these people, they're nowhere to be found.

These people also struggle to pay their booth rent. Barbering is a hobby to them, not a career. The moves they make are not intentional because they don't really want to work. Being consistent forces them to be held accountable.

GET OFF YO PHONE

If your phone is not generating at least one thousand dollars a week, get outside and hustle. Staying on your phone the entire work shift is senseless. It's sad that adults have become addicted to a phone that is not generating any money for them. Phones are a great tool and definitely needed for business. However, if you are routinely not working, sitting and staring or scrolling up and down on your phone is a waste of time.

Maximize the time you have at work. If you have no clients for that day, go out and get some. The phone is not the answer. The time you spend worrying about what is coming in, you could be going out and getting it. Although, the phone helps speed up some interactions, that's not always the case. The real interaction comes from face to face contact. In the meantime, stay off your phone when your client is in your chair. Don't be on your phone when you are in the middle of a service. Clients don't like when they don't have your full attention. Also, being on the phone while having a client in your chair is rude and unprofessional. Being on the phone during a service can be the most annoying thing to a client. People don't come in to hear your entire conversation with someone else. Long conversations can wait until after the service is done. Unless it is an emergency, it can wait. If you need to step out, excuse yourself to handle your business and return in a timely manner.

SOCIAL MEDIA BRANDING

Social media branding is a great way to expose others to who you are and the work you do. With a good product or service, your business can explode fairly quickly.

Social media has given barbers, artists, stylists, personal trainers, chefs, and other professions a platform to grow their businesses and reach people from across the world in a way that has never been done before. The more followers you have, the bigger your brand can be. The biggest thing with social media is your reach, engagement, and brand awareness. Having a great social media presence can lead to endorsements or brand ambassador opportunities. Once you hit that status, people really respect your craft and you become a recognized influencer.

The job of a brand ambassador or influencer is to endorse certain products on their social media page. In return, a company typically sends free products and promotes you on their social media page as well. The power of influence is real.

Let's be real though. The power of social media has some people confused about where they really are in life. Some people are addicted to likes and attention over actual real business. Social media presence or likes does not always equate to money being spent with you. That's what you call vanity numbers. Vanity numbers will not grow your business, but foot traffic will. It's not smart to solely rely on social media for marketing. It's better to have an assortment of ways to brand and market yourself.

TRADEMARK YOUR BRAND

If you want to solidify yourself as a brand, you have to trademark your logo. A trademark is a type of intellectual property consisting of a recognizable sign, design, or expression which distinguishes products or services of a particular source from those of others. Trademarks used to identify services are usually called service marks.

The trademark owner can be an individual, business, organization, or any legal entity. A trademark may be located on a package, a label, a voucher, or on the product itself. Trademarking your brand is a good idea, especially if you plan on being in business for a long time. Without trademarking your business or ideas, you run the risk of someone stealing your brand identity. If you work hard to build something, you want to protect it as much as you can. Your brand is your shield. It's your name and your reputation.

Trademarking your logo or business allows you to franchise your brand or business legally. Once your business is established, it opens the door for more opportunities. Going to a graphic designer and having him or her create a logo is just the beginning of having a legitimate brand or business. There are so many people out there that will steal your ideas and make it their own. So many times, small business owners don't invest the extra funds into making sure their business is legit. Even though you may be a small business, does not mean you can't run it like a Fortune 500 corporation. Some individuals will be in business for years and never own their brand. That makes no sense. Take the time and invest in your brand, business, and your future. If you work hard for something, protect it.

GET A BUSINESS ACCOUNT

Your personal account and business account should be two separate entities. Don't mix business with pleasure. Set up your LLC. Once you have an EIN (Employer Identification Number), you can open a business bank account.

Having a business account is pivotal for your life and business. Your proof of income and taxes will be filed based on the activities within your business account. Some independent contractors don't get business accounts or file taxes. However, when it's time to make a major purchase, you won't have proof of income and your only option may be trying to purchase it under someone else name. That's no way to operate your life or your business.

Opening a business account is simple. Go to any financial institution, meet with a business planner or associate, and discuss ways to grow your business. Get yourself set-up for the future. After you incorporate your business, get your EIN, and set-up the bank account, hire a CPA (certified public accountant) for your taxes. A CPA will keep you organized with your financial transactions. A CPA can help you not overspend, watch what's coming in, watch what's going out, etc.

You should also consider your ability to establish credit through your business. Business credit may be what you need to secure your own location, add more team members, increase your marketing, or build your infrastructure because business credit gives you access to trade lines and business credit cards.

BRAND VS. UNBRANDED

A branded shop is a shop that normally has a theme or unique look to it. Shops that are brands are normally more organized, professional, and stylish. A shop that is branded cares about its reputation and how it treats customers. A traditional barbershop can be a number of things. A brand normally has a manger or receptionist to answer calls and book appointments. Unfortunately, in some of the unbranded shops, anything goes seems to be the mindset. In an unbranded barbershop, there is normally no manger, the aesthetics are basic, the customer service is poor, and the reputation proceeds that. Normally, the owner of an unbranded shop wants to get his money and doesn't care about anything else. A branded shop presents a certain atmosphere. The vibe and energy at a branded location are different.

Brands bring money. Unbranded shops operate like trap houses—no real rules. Anything goes. Many unbranded shops don't have a manager which raises issues. Not all independent contractors will meet the professional requirements you want in your establishment. So when you introduce multiple personalities in a room with no structure or guidance, it could lead to distraction and devastation for your business.

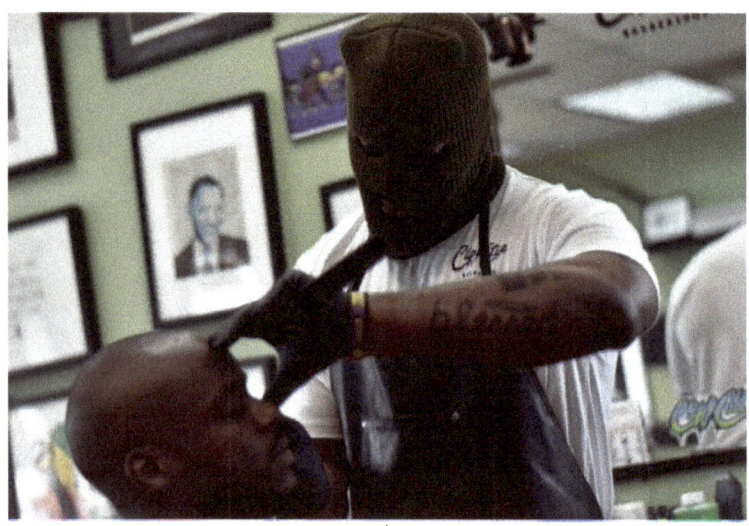

RESPECT THE BUSINESS

Don't try to pimp the business. Pimping the business means coming in to take walk-ins during peak times and then leaving. The business is there for you when you need it so be there for the business when it needs you. Show support to your fellow co-workers. Be a team player. Don't come in the business with the attitude that you don't really rock with the people in it. Your energy is loud and people can feel it. Keep the same energy you had when interviewing and asking for the opportunity. Instead of doing less, see how you can be of help. Be encouraging to your co-workers. Respect the rules of the business.

To show ultimate respect to the business, you have to first make sure it is a good fit for you. If the morals and values of the business do not align with your core values, do not apply. Sometimes it's about much more than a few dollars. Don't inquire about a place just to get some money. However, coming into the business and trying to change the structure and rules, is not right either. Independent contractors go to new businesses for opportunities to better themselves. Independent contractors tend to complain about the lack of structure of their previous place of employment however, when they get to a new location, after about two months, they don't like the structure of that business either. Reality is, you cannot pick and choose the rules and structure of someone else's business. Either it works for you or it doesn't. The owner of every establishment had to spend time and money to put their vision together. The mission and vision of the business has to be honored and respected.

S.A.L.E. = START THE SALE. ASK QUESTIONS. LEAD PEOPLE TO BUY. END THE SALE.

As an independent contractor, you are a sales person. Every time you interact with someone, you are selling yourself. You start any sale by introducing yourself. Then, the focus should be on the other person. What are you trying to learn? What do you need to know to move the sale forward/ Ask questions because they help you understand what that person wants or needs. Leading someone to buy means you are either convincing someone to buy or they are already sold on what you have to offer.

Ending the sale is the most important. When you end any sale, you want the other person to have all of your contact information, time of availability, and how you can be reached. The goal is to have as many people as possible come back and refer others to you. Every form of entrepreneurship involves sales. Sales is how business thrive. Selling yourself to a customer is always the biggest hurdle. People are going to spend money with someone they relate to. You as a salesperson, must adapt to each client without changing who you are.

Everyone likes someone relatable and trustworthy. One of the easiest ways to start a sale is to ask someone who cuts their hair. Always have your business card in hand. You never know when you might meet your next client. Can you sell yourself to people? Practice your sales pitch in the mirror sometimes. Some barbers and stylists have talent, but lack interpersonal skills. However, that doesn't mean you shouldn't work at it. Get your sales pitch together. Practice greeting people. Make eye contact.

Give firm handshakes. If you believe in your skills and want to grow, you have to figure out how to talk to people. Just doing the service itself is not enough.

BURNING OUT

Sometimes you have to take a break for yourself. Short breaks are good. Breaks are also healthy for your body and your mind. When you are constantly on the go, you run a huge risk of burning out.

Sometimes, we as independent contractors give our clients all of our energy and time. We have to give some of that energy and time to ourselves, as well. Nobody can take care of you better than you and there is nothing wrong with pampering yourself. The human mind naturally needs a break. Going hard in the paint is great, but vacations are even better. If you work hard, you should be able to enjoy the fruits of your labor.

When you are burnt out, your tolerance is lower, temper is shorter, patience is thin, and sometimes your work suffers from it. Regularly, we need moments to refresh, recharge, and reflect on what we are doing, where we are going, and how we are going to get there. Sometimes, you can't see it by standing in the same spot. You are not going to be in the mood every day to perform. It's just impossible to always have the desire to want to work. You're human, not a robot. So, give yourself time to rest. Your mind, body, and business will thank you for it.

LEAD GENERATION CALLS

From time to time, give old customers a call, email, or text to let them know you are thinking about them. Also, every blue moon, send them a discount code on a product or service you're providing. People love discounts and feeling valued—it's the small things that count.

In a business like barbering, it's all about relationships. It's important to get customers locked in, especially in the beginning. Set a small goal for yourself. Send a text, call, or email to twenty-five people every two weeks so you are touching base with your clients. Clients appreciate the communication. Someone might not have been thinking about a haircut until they get your message. Now you've made yourself top-of-mind. In your calls, texts, and emails, convey how you appreciate them as your client. Also, use the opportunity to ask what styles they may be interested in getting in the future. Once you have a better understanding of your client, you can better service them.

Lead generation calls will help grow and sustain your business. During your calls, ask current clients for the names of potential new clients so you can put them on your call, text, and email list. Once they know about you, where you are located, and what your skills are, your opportunities are endless. The best part about lead generation calls—they require no cash outlay. It's a free form of marketing and promoting yourself. It costs you nothing to do and entrepreneurs should take advantage of it.

SLOW MOTION BETTER THAN NO MOTION

Slow motion is always better than no motion. The objective is to keep your chain in rotation. However, you will have slow days which aren't all bad. Those are the days where you go and run your errands and market yourself. Make use of your time.

If you are having a slow day, that is the time to think about ways to improve. You could clean up, pass out flyers, or reflect. Even if you have one to three clients in a day, that's okay. Getting something is better than nothing at all. Slow days are sometimes good for resting, as well. When it's super busy, you are going to miss those slow moments. So, appreciate the slow days while you have them.

Normally, after a busy week, the following week may be a bit slower. Slow days are when you do the chores at the shop. Slow days are when you spend time to get to know your coworkers. Maybe take a lunch with your work crew. Slow days are the time to walk around your plaza and get to know your work neighbors. Slow days are for building relationships and networking with others. A slow day can still be productive. Just because it wasn't as financially beneficial as you may have wanted, doesn't mean you can't get other things done. Your goal is to make the most of out every day...even slow ones.

WALK-IN FLOW

Is just what it sounds like—a flow. Do not depend on the walk-in flow because when the walk-in flow dries up, you are done. The flow comes in waves. If you are solely dependent on that, your money will come in waves, which no one wants.

The walk-in flow is determined by many things such as weather, day of the month, holidays, time of day, etc. There are various factors that play into the walk-in flow. That's why you can't depend on it. The only thing you should depend on is your own hustle. Walk-ins come and go, but your hustle is forever. Traffic flow is always sporadic and a bit unpredictable. You will always have your peak times, but you cannot depend on that. Walk-ins are people who are in need of a service without an appointment. As long as there is a need for your services, you will be around. People are always willing to give someone a first chance. You must be present and available when the walk-ins come in. Some people prefer to remain walk-ins and not planned appointments due to their schedule. Some businesses have better walk-in traffic because of location. Some businesses have good walk-in traffic because of reputation and customer service. Walk-in traffic is important to every business because you as an independent contractor need those opportunities to grow your business.

SWEAT EQUITY

Sweat equity is a party's contribution to a project in the form of labor, as opposed to financial equity such as paying others to perform the task. Sweat equity has an application in business. For example, where the owners put in effort to build the business, and the independent contractors reap the benefits. Sweat equity is the grunt work usually laid down by the owner.

The owners should lay the foundation and structure of the business. However, the owner shouldn't have to do ALL the work on his/her own. If you are coming into an establishment, bring something to the table, don't just eat off the table. When the owner does all the marketing, promotions, management, job posting, hiring, etc. that's a lot on one person's plate already. It's up to the independent contractor to do his or her part and go out there and get it. It's not the owner's responsibility to get and keep building your clientel.

It's not always cool to eat off the owner's overflow either. Just because the owner has clients that he or she can't always get to doesn't mean you should depend on that volume. The person who built the brand/business is giving you an opportunity to showcase your skills. Most owners want to share their platform with someone who deserves it. There is a great value to sweat equity so don't be afraid to get your hands dirty and do the tough work for the business.

BUSINESS CARDS

Business cards are a pivotal part of business. It's just that simple. You are not ready to do business without business cards. Your business cards should be on your desk station, door, and wallet.

As an entrepreneur, be ready for business at all times. You never know who you might meet. Your next interaction with someone can lead to a long-lasting relationship. If you provide a service to someone and don't guarantee they have at least two ways to contact you, you are losing out on a potential repeat customer.

Communication is key to gaining clients. Some barbers and stylists do a service and don't give out a card, then get mad when the client returns without an appointment. Tell people how they can reach you, book with you, or communicate with you through your business cards. When you go to events, gatherings, concerts, etc., have that card on you. Whenever tons of people gather in one spot, that is the time to capitalize because you never know who you will meet. If you stay ready you don't have to get ready. Be ready to meet new people.

While considered somewhat old-fashioned, business cards are still very effective.

LEARN AND GROW

Regardless of your industry, learn and grow. Once you learn, you should be able to earn. Learning and growing are inevitable. Even if you have no intentions of doing either, you will.

Allow yourself to evolve or risk becoming outdated and left behind. You can't bend or slow down time. And with time changing, so does everything else. Don't be afraid to move with the change. Try to be better, do better, improve in every way you can. There will always be new, innovative, and hungry talent coming behind you. Someone is always looking to take your spot so add more skills to your resume. The more you can do, the better you will be. You never know how you can use those skills elsewhere.

Also, keep in mind that you can learn from anybody. It might be learning what to do or even what *not* to do from someone you worked with in the past. You should learn at least one thing from every business/location. From management style and customer service to processes and operations, there is always something to learn.

ROOKIES SHOULD OUTWORK THE VETS

No matter the occupation, rookies should outwork the veterans. The rookies may not be able to outperform the vets, but they should be able to outwork them.

When you are new to an environment or industry, you should be the first to arrive at work and the last one to leave. Rookies need to come in with new energy and keep the vets on their toes. At the same time, rookies should soak up any knowledge (game) that they can get from the vets.

In the beginning, you are supposed to come in to get a feel for the business and how it operates. Your opportunities may come slow at first, but, if you stay down until you come up, you will prosper. When you are a rookie, you need to be ready and available for any task. Being a rookie is about building a foundation and learning. Rookies get the latitude to make more mistakes. Some rookies will have more talent than vets. However, stay humble. Always remain teachable. There will be many questions to ask. However, if you put your time in, you will master it. As a rookie, be fearless. Don't let certain obstacles deter you from reaching new heights. Friend with a purpose. Outwork everyone. Do things like you got a point to prove. Your rookie year will be tough because there is a steep learning curve. However, if you can get through your rookie year, you can accomplish anything.

QUALITY VS. QUANTITY

Being an entrepreneur is about your reach. It's a volume game. However, doing numbers is great, but does your quality match? When your quality and quantity match, you have the chance to make a lot of money. People love to shop with you when you are fast, efficient, convenient, and at a reasonable price.

Some barbers and stylists focus on quantity without producing adequate quality. That's not a system built to last. You have to find a balance as there is no substitute for quality.

Quality looks better, lasts longer, and takes real skill to produce.

Quality *is the standard of something as measured against other things of similar kind; the degree of excellence of something.*

Quantity is *the amount or number of material or immaterial thing not usually estimated by spatial measurement.*

You have to have a certain amount of talent about yourself to produce quality. Quality takes more time, practice, and patience to execute. Quantity is good for your pockets. It's a good feeling when you can achieve both—now you're working with something.

As an independent contractor, you want to create high demand for yourself. When that demand is buzzing, that means people like the product, respect the product, and will buy the product. Quality work speaks for itself. People will pay good money for quality. What you want to create is residual income for yourself. You can get that residual income if you put in the work to separate yourself from everyone else. You get out what you put in.

WRITE IT DOWN, TRACK YOUR NUMBERS

Keep track of your numbers. Keeping track of your numbers is how you will be able to track your progress. If you don't log on, write down how many clients you see every day. If not, you will lose track of your scheduling and the amount of money you are making. Writing things down allows you to be more organized. Being organized is the key to success.

Tracking your numbers allows you to set goals for yourself. If you know what you did each day, week, or month, you can better manage how you approach your goals. If you are not writing anything down, you don't know how much you are making and you won't be able to plan. If you struggle with staying organized, it's best to buy a notebook or organizer so you can start tracking your records. Organization will be better for your life. You will be able to know when you will start, take a break, and end your day. If you ever get off track, you can resort back to your daily planner. Writing everything down keeps you prepared for the next. If you don't write things down or record it, you will never have anything to measure it against. When your business is structured, you can wake up every day knowing how best to spend your time that day.

EXIT STRATEGY/PLAN

Don't leave the business without getting everything you need out of it. Many entrepreneurs walk away from their business without ever reaching the financial goals they set for themselves. If you have been doing something for a long time, you should be in a far better position than you were when you started.

In any field, there's going to be a start point and an end point. No one necessarily plans to do something forever. Make the most of your time in a location. Set goals, accomplish them, and move on to the next. However, when it's all said and done, what you did with your time and money are most important.

Save, invest, make smart financial decisions because you never want to look back over your times as a business owner and not see financial growth or even simply, finances. Don't leave with less than you started with. Invest in a working with someone who specializes in financial planning, credit, and investments. Be smart about how you navigate your present so you can be confident about your future.

STRUCTURE

Structure is pivotal for business. The way the foundation of a business is set up will tell you everything. A good structured system will help you thrive. Although some independent contractors like structure, others don't. Those who like structure usually prefer a routine because it gives them stability and even predictability. Someone who likes stability and structure is normally thinking long-term.

Structure is the arrangement of and relation between the parts of elements of something complex. Some people lack structure and discipline but structure is fundamental to a balanced life. Being all over the place or not knowing what you are going to do is not how to live. Without structure, you have no sense of direction. You will never grow without structure.

PROTECT THE BRAND

Protecting the brand extends across everything—haircuts, customer service, professionalism, and dependability. If one bad apple is not in alignment with the business and its values, it could bring the entire establishment down. Protect the brand at all cost. That means if someone has to go, it is what it is. The brand has a reputation to uphold and no individual should be able to compromise that, it must be stopped. The reputation effects everyone involved. You don't need bad press or bad publicity surrounding your name or business.

TAKING A LEAP

Taking a leap requires faith, perseverance, and calculated risks. Results don't happen in comfort zones. In order to get ahead, we must progress. We must take a leap. You can't do epic things with basic people. So, some will be left behind. Taking a leap won't always be easy, but it is necessary for growth. If you have been doing something the same way for a long time with no results, it may be time to switch things up. Taking a leap may have you nervous, doubtful, and confused. However, it is <u>*necessary*</u>.

STOP FALLING FOR EVERY SOCIAL MEDIA GIMMICK

Every social media gimmick is not for you. What works for one person may not be for you. Keeping up with trends is fine, but don't abandon what keeps you paid for every new trend that comes along. There are leaders in our industry who charge thousands of dollars to educate others. While that's one option, it may be better or you to simply walk over to a colleague's booth and get the same information. With so much advance technology, you can self-teach yourself more than you know. I believe paying thousands of dollars for knowledge that may be available for free is absurd. That's just my two cents.

A WISE MAN LEARNS FROM HIS MISTAKES. A WISER MAN LEARNS FROM OTHERS' MISTAKES

Sometimes you can learn what *not* to do by watching the mistakes of others and avoid taking the same path. Be aware. Be assertive. If you see that something doesn't work, take heed and adjust. Some mishaps and mistakes were laid out for you to witness and learn from. Not doing the things you see others fail at will make you stronger. Some people see others make mistakes and try to attempt the same thing only to also fail. Those failures were sent as a warning for a reason. Don't hurt yourself with the same foolishness. Growth is key. Once you know, you should grow. Once you learn, you should earn. Be mindful of all the obstacles that have been set before you so when they present themselves again, you know how to play it.

SETUP A SEPARATE WAY FOR BOOTH RENTERS TO PAY YOU

People don't like paying bills. When bother renters have to pay owners directly, they feel as though they are making the owner rich. However, they will be paying the same booth rent to someone else at some point. The problem is, people count your money without thinking about what expenses you may occur.

It takes money to run a business. Booth renters don't think about the overhead involved in building and maintaining a business. To separate any potential tension between booth renters and the owner, set up an online site where booth renters can pay directly. Make the transactions less personal. Paying the booth rent online keeps things more structured and formal.

COLLABORATE VS. COMPETE

We all have talents and gifts. How we use our gifts determines our direction and final end point. Sometimes entrepreneurs don't work together because they fear making someone else bigger. However, we all need each other to survive. Collab don't compete.

When we collaborate with one another, beautiful things can happen. All participants get credit for the success. Competing against one another takes too much time and energy. Don't get it twisted, being competitive is not a bad thing. However, let's push each other so we can become better. Instead of worrying about who's ahead, let's come up with ideas to both get paid. Let's brainstorm. Let's create a vision board. All boats can rise, together.

More doors open when you team up. You might become an influencer and can partner with another influencer, creating a winning situation. Don't shortchange yourself by thinking you can do everything by yourself. Work well with others and everything else will more easily fall into place.

BE ABOUT YOUR COMMUNITY

Get out, get active, be social. True entrepreneurs get out in the community to talk with the people in the town, schools, restaurants, and local businesses. In order to grow, you have to have a sense of community. A community sticks together. When you are involved in a community, people stick together. Whenever there is an event in your community, go. Check out what is going on at that particular event. Being a part of the community also gives you a chance to network. You may meet other entrepreneurs or get be able to share new ideas to help improve your business. Expand your network by registering your business with the local chamber of commerce. Most chambers of commerce allow you the opportunity to do a ribbon cutting event, place your business in the local paper, and keep you in the loop for upcoming events. Also, if there are any football, basketball, charity, networking, events—go!

WHAT'S YOUR MOTIVATION?

What motivates you to do what you do? What propels you to get out of bed in the morning? Is it for your kids and family? Are you chasing greatness? What's your legacy going to be? Those are the questions you have to ask yourself as an entrepreneur.

Different things fuel us all, but in order to be great, you have to be cut from a different cloth. When you are driving for greatness, outside of the normal things motivate you. You don't want average, basic, or mediocre. Motivation is the driving force behind a lot of successful people. Most of them were wired differently. Motivation comes with goals and purpose. Your goals and purpose will keep your motivation on track.

Every once in a while, the best of us can get side-tracked. However, when you have a solid base, motivation, and goals, you have your foundation to fall back on. When you're motivated to accomplish certain goals, nothing stands in your way of getting shit done. For motivation, use the people that counted you out or hated on you. It all adds fuel to the fire. Use all obstacles, good or bad, as motivation to keep you moving forward on your path.

GOOD VIDES ONLY

Just like bad vides are contagious, so are good vibes. Good vibes and positive energy work. People feed off positive energy because it's like light. Bad vibes and bad energy are like darkness. Whatever you spread is what you are going to get back.

Focus on the positive things you have going in your life. Smile sometimes smiling is contagious too. When you have good vibes and good energy about yourself, you attract more people. Sometimes positive vibe people irk the spirit out of negative vibe people. They can only see negative things so that's what they spread. Positive vibe individuals are normally accomplishing things, have good news to spread, and are willing to help others when they can. Negative energy will mess up the money. Positive vibes bring more money.

How you look at life and approach life is totally up to you. Good vibes are like fresh air. It feels good. Good vibes make you feel like you can accomplish anything. Good vibes bring you inspiration. Sometimes that's all people need to get them motivated about something. Negative energy can spread like a wildfire. If you start experiencing negative energy, pull away from that person because you don't want that seeping into your mindset. Good vibes only.

CREATE YOUR OWN CONTENT

Be your #1 fan. Support your own dreams because your dreams will be as big as you push them to be. Be creative, be fearless, be original. Fresh, new content is always appreciated. You don't need anybody's permission to be dope on your own.

Create your own content about your brand and ways to improve it. Write out different content. Whatever you push out into the world, make sure it's authentic. People can feel when something is not original or you are trying too hard. If you are having trouble with creating your own content, get with a marketing strategist to come up with various ways to promote yourself. Everything is about engagement now. Do you have a good product or service that people want and need? How do you promote it? A lot of people are doing the same things, but how good your product is and how it is presented makes the difference. When you are promoting something, it needs to be clear what it is. People must understand what your brand really is. If people don't understand who you are and what you do, they will not buy from you. Your pictures, angles, and clarity matter. Do your best to keep all background space clean at all times. The focus should always be on the product.

When you have talent and it's presented well, you can thrive. Find your lane. Operate in your space. Your superpower is what you do in a way that no one else can. That's what makes you unique. When you can do the same as others and still stand out, that's greatness. Build your content around what you do best.

KNOW YOUR AUDIENCE

When you know your audience, cater to them. You have to give them what they want. Don't start promoting other ventures that have nothing to do with your original product. If you are going to start a new business venture, make sure the product or service is related to what you are already doing. Trying to expand with something that has nothing to do with your niche can be very challenging. If you are planning to switch up your main source of income to something else, make sure you do research about the new option(s) before investing. Everything always starts with your base. Once you have mastered all you can in a particular field, it's okay to expand. Just make sure it does not impact your first business. You have to know your audience and in turn, your audience has to know you. Don't confuse them with a lack of focus.

ETHICS...GET SOME

People come together to work from different places and different backgrounds. However, that's no excuse to be cutthroat. Sometimes small business entrepreneurs operate in a cutthroat fashion because they are thirsty for money. When you are doing what you are supposed to be, you won't have to worry about doing something cutthroat for money.

Being cutthroat can ruin a lot of relationships. You have to keep in mind when you make cutthroat moves it can affect everyone you work with. Cutthroat moves are selfish moves. If you work with someone every day, don't make selfish moves that will jeopardize the dynamic or have people looking at you sideways. Realistically, when you make cutthroat moves, you put everything at risk. The money you receive for a cutthroat move is temporary. But the relationships with your team, coworker, crew are forever. Don't have an "I got to get mine first" mentality. Nothing is wrong with wanting to have things, but the way you go about getting the things you have makes a difference. You can't be happy with your riches, if you're piss poor morally. Cutthroat moves start fights, break up relationships, and cause overall confusion and tension. At the end of the day, it's not worth it.

CAPITALIZING

Is your business growing on its own? We are all in business to make a profit. Never be content with making just enough. This is a capitalistic society. We are entrepreneurs should all strive to capitalize on your business. When you are not, you got to keep it going. When you are hot, you are hot. You have to ride the wave. Some people reach a certain level of success, then stop. They think they are good. That's the wrong way to go about things. The truth is, when your demand is high, you have to kill it every time. There may come a day when you do slow down, but while you can get it, don't stop. You never know what type of obstacles may come your way in the future. When life and circumstances change, you have to change with it. If you stack everything up high when the slow times do come, you are prepared. Now, you are not panicking because you didn't build your base first.

CULTURE

The culture of an organization is important and so is determining a business's core values. Leaders should be clear on what their company stands for. You should know your impact on the community, the strengths and weaknesses of your operations, the goal of the company and even, where the business will be in three to five years.

WHAT'S YOUR PORTFOLIO/PROFILE

Where is your work showcased? How can someone get an idea of your skills without ever meeting you in person? Instagram, Facebook Market Place, Styleseat? Those are all options for people to find examples of your work.

These days, examples of your work need to be easily accessible because not everyone trusts walking into a shop and having a great experience. They want to understand what they'll likely experience. So, you should make it easy for them to get to know you and what you're capable of doing for them. Whatever platform you use, take full advantage of every opportunity. Make sure people can see what you do, understand what you do, and book with you.

FEEDBACK

Feedback is good. Constructive criticism helps you get where you need to go. Too many times, people take constructive feedback the wrong way. Maybe it's the way the information is presented. However, feedback keeps you balanced. Feedback doesn't allow you to be wrong about something and keep it moving. Feedback gives you positive reassurance of the things you are doing well, too.

We all need feedback. We all need someone in our corner that is going to keep it real with us. No one person knows everything. No one person does everything correctly. Constructive feedback holds us accountable for our actions.

FIRST IMPRESSIONS

You only have one opportunity to make a first impression so make it a good one. Your appearance is everything. Your prices must coordinate in how you look and carry yourself. Charging premium prices but coming to work looking homeless is incongruent. It doesn't line up.

If you dress for success, you don't have to worry about those type of issues. What you do outside of work is fine. However, you have to keep in mind that everybody is not into your outside lifestyle. So, don't let your outside lifestyle spill over into work.

When you meet someone for the first time, you want to make sure your posture, energy, and appearance is on point.

That is going to set the tone for how the rest of the interaction will go. The atmosphere is also a very important component. Making sure your work station is clean and clear of debris makes a difference. People like walking into an atmosphere that's inviting to all. Everything from the appropriate television shows to watch and music to play are important. While you can't make everyone happy, it's better to be safe than sorry. First impressions may determine if someone is a one-time customer or a repeat customer.

FREELANCE OR FREE LOADER?

Most people take on the freelance approach is only looking to free load. These types of people normally don't stay in any place too long. They want to come in whenever, leave whenever, and take whatever they can get their hands on. That's not fair to the business. You can't stop someone with this mindset. However, if you own an establishment you can definitely cut ties with this person. The freelancer wants to build up enough clients so they can get money quickly and go. No plans on building a real relationship with the customers. If you want to be a freelancer, you should just be mobile and gain clients that way. Working in an establishment is not for you. There is nothing wrong with being a freelancer, just make sure you are doing it off your own merit.

PUT YO NAME AND NUMBER IN EVERYBODY PHONE

When you are trying to build a clientele, one of the best ways to do so is to add your name and number to their contacts. After every service is complete, give that individual your name, phone number, your availability and how to book with you in the future. As an entrepreneur, you have to dig into the psychology of how people think. People are creatures of habits. So, if you can provide an exceptional service and you make booking convenient, you can build a strong client base. Once your information is in somebody's phone, it normally stays there. People tend to scroll up and down in their phone. If they see your number over and over again, they are going to eventually use it. The human mind normally gravitates to what it continually sees.

FACE TO FACE MARKETING

When you have a love for people, raw and authentic marketing, such as face-to-face marketing, is easy. You get a chance to convince people because they see you right on the spot. As a hustler, there's no better feeling than turning a customer into a client in the same day. People buy into who you are as a person.

One of the main aspects of entrepreneurship is sales. Can you sell yourself to someone? If you can't, you are not ready to be an entrepreneur. In-person marketing is about the art of the sale. The rush of talking to people. When you become good at it, nothing is more rewarding. You meet so many people when you are out and about. Being able to talk to strangers is a gift. It relies on the basics. That's how you start the relationship and it's pretty cool to meet people randomly and connect with them. We are all connected to each other in some sort of way. We as entrepreneurs have to continue to connect with others.

DIRECT APPROACH

If you are an owner of a business, you have to use a direct approach with independent contractors under your brand. Set the ground rules early. This protects you because they will never be able to feign ignorance of the rules. Every business should have a handbook and an independent contractor agreement. When you bring someone onto the team, go over the information with them thoroughly. Review every single detail and key point. Your business is the platform they are operating under so what you expect form them as an owner should be understood from the start.

Avoid having someone come in trying to change the rules of the business or claiming they didn't understand the guidelines. Also, don't have your vets thinking the business rules don't apply to them after a certain point. It's a constant struggle for owners to keep everyone on the same page. However, as the owner, you have to set the foundation and manage throughout. Owners have to remain firm in the principles of their business. There is nothing wrong with considering new ideas, but don't restructure your entire business for one person who can't follow instructions.

Monitor newcomers and start with a trial period to ensure they know how to follow the rules. Answer their questions and provide as much guidance as possible. Once the trial period is over, they should know and understand what the business is about.

EMPATHIC LISTENING

Empathic listening is the ability to understand and share the feelings of another. When you have a love for people, you are able to understand what they are going through. You empathize with them. Some clients tend to expect you to be a listening ear. Essentially, you are a therapist of some sort. People trust you with their most confidential information. Your job is to listen, don't judge, and give feedback if that's what they want.

We all learn from each other's experiences. Empathic listening could help you with a future situation. You may have never been through something before, but because you listen to someone else's story, it could help you in the end. Empathic listening has to be something that's part of your character. You can't always take the money and not get to know your clients in some kind of way. People will tell you what they want to know. You don't have to be all in their business to find out either. Your business is built on clients and maintaining them is based on strong relationships. Don't make them feel like a number. You don't have to be their best friend, but don't make them feel like they are insignificant. Some of the least-skilled people have decent clientele based on how they treat people. They treat their people well and it shows.

HOW TO RESPOND GRACEFULLY

When the chips are down, how do you respond? Everything does not always go as planned. Life is about wins and losses. You are going to win sometimes and you are going to lose sometimes. How you respond to either situation is the important part.

Don't be a sore loser. When something does not go your way, take your L's like an adult. There is honor in a loss. As long as you give something, you can live with the results. As an entrepreneur, every week will not be popping. That's not realistic. When things aren't going right, how you respond says a lot about you. Tough times are going to happen, but tough people outlast tough times. When chips are falling down find other ways to be resourceful. Tap into your gifts. Take the time to work on other projects. As long as you are being productive in some kind of way, you are fine. When you have that down time, appreciate it. Sometimes it's good to step back, relax, and regroup. As long as you are continually investing into yourself, you can never lose. In the meantime, if you invest in yourself, when things pick back up, you will have made more progress than your peers. The results of your hard work will show up. At all times, remain humble. Don't get caught up in who you think you are and what you have achieved in the past. If you live by cheers, you will die by the boos. Don't let compliments get you too gassed and criticism get you down. Know who you are as a person. Know what it is that you are trying to accomplish and if it does not feed your spirit, walk away.

EVEN WHEN YOU LOSE THE PASSION, YOU STILL GOT TO WORK

Some days you are not going to have the passion to do the thing you love the most. However, you have to push through it. Days when you are not feeling it, you will have to dig deep to make it happen. Get out of your feelings and get this money. The show must go on. If you need a break to cool off, take one. Even if you need an extended lunch break, take one. In the meantime, not working or hustling at all is not an option. You will never hear a hustler say he doesn't want to hustle no more. Push past whatever it is you are going through and make it happen. If you give up, you'll never know what you could have done. However, if you keep going, you'll look back one day and be grateful that you never folded. Passion can come and go sometimes. It's natural to lose the passion for something you love over time. The thing is, you have to stick with it though. Some days are going to be tougher than others.

When passion fails, that's when work ethic kicks in. If you don't have a strong work ethic, you are bound to fall when the passion wanes. Any time you are doing something for money, it's a business. Business always comes first. Business and passion can get mixed up sometimes, but if you balance it out, you will survive.

FINANCE BEFORE ROMANCE

Dating an entrepreneur is rough. Or schedules are unpredictable and sometimes, so is our money. When you are an entrepreneur, you are a true hunter. You are always looking for your next kill. Romance and all that mushy stuff often takes a backseat. You have to be focused on your business so you can operate at your best.

Love is a beautiful thing, but love don't pay the bills. Skills pay the bills. When you are at the top of your game as an entrepreneur, everyone wants a piece of you. It's like everyone wants to know who you are. You're kinda like a rockstar of some sort because not everyone is successful as an entrepreneur. You become very desirable when you are winning. However, you must be careful in who you entertain. It's a benefit to someone else when they don't bring what you bring to the table. Otherwise, after a while, you began to feel used or that person is just an expense.

Entrepreneurs don't have a 9 to 5. It's more like a first client to the last client operation. Your days end when you run out of clients for the day. Planning dates, movies, and meet ups can be a bit tough. But you have to find a way to make time for the other person. Dating a person who is not as busy as you can be a problem sometimes because that person typically wants more of your time than what you are willing to give. Dating a person just as busy or busier than you can also cause issues because neither of you have time for one another. There has to be a balance to your relationship in order for it to work.

At the end of the day, look at the purse first. Money isn't everything, but it matters when you don't have it. Dating someone who doesn't have it like that is one thing, but dating someone who don't want shit is a whole other set of problems. Entrepreneurs get your finances together as much as you can before you settle down. Work as much as you can in the beginning so you can enjoy the fruits of your labor differently with your partner. Invest in your business first so it can grow. The right person will come along at the right time to help you grow financially and personally, later. Don't throw all your money away dating, partying, and bullshitting. All that stuff will be there. Get your finances together first. You will have more options after that anyway.

Life is a big math equation. Addition vs. subtraction. Either you are a liability or an asset. Can you add to my life or are you taking away from my life? It's very simple. You don't want to have to make all your permanent moves through someone else.

DON'T THINK ABOUT A STOREFONT UNTIL YOU HAVE AN OVERFLOW

If you don't have an overflow, don't even think about a shop. A physical location requires time, money, and overflow. Don't jump the gun and accumulate debt trying to open a storefront. It may seem easy, but it requires a lot of work and is tons of responsibility. Plus, certain products and services don't require a physical location and instead, an online store is all you need.

If you are a master chef, personal trainer, photographer, mechanic, barber, or stylist, opening a storefront should be tied to an overflow of clients. You need enough clients to sustain yourself. The type of business will dictate the cost. I estimate a minimum of $25K for new equipment, $25K for a certified contractor, and a minimum of $25K in reserve cash in case something goes wrong. Don't forget to also consider money for marketing, branding, repairs, flyers, cards, etc.

After you get everything in place, you still have to maintain it which comes with its own costs and considerations. Operate as though you don't have booth renters and ask yourself if you're in the financial position to cover the expenses on your own. If the answer is yes, make the best decision for your business.

PEOPLE BUY INTO YOU WHEN THEY KNOW YOUR STORY

People relate to the struggle. They want to feel like they connect to you. Everyone has a story. Some stories are more relatable and inspiring than others. Sometimes your story is what attracts people to you. Tell people a little bit about yourself and keep in mind, you don't have to give them everything. However, let people feel you out somewhat.

You may have a story that people can relate to or one that can inspire others. You just never know who you may meet or how a relationship can be formed. Clients also give you their testimonial as well. There may be something that happened in their life that could help change or model a new perspective in your life. We all can grow and learn from one another. As time moves, forward, we build bonds with people that may last forever. The bonds that you build will always be more fulfilling than the money you make. It's a people-driven business. If you don't love people, you have no business in the service industry. The people give you the energy sometimes to press on. Therefore, share your stories. Engage with the people you serve. Build long-lasting relationships.

BE GRATEFUL FOR EVERY CLIENT

Saying thank you goes a long way. Be appreciative of every opportunity because you never know how many you will have. Do every service to the best of your ability. We sometimes lose sight of how many people we service in a day, week, or month. Always work hard and stay humble. You will be rewarded in more ways than one.

Some entrepreneurs star off humble in the beginning when they have no clients. However, once they build a sustainable clientele, they start treating their clients with disregard. That's not cool or anyway to be. Being arrogant is the quickest way to lose it all. Don't get it twisted, clients have no right to try and take advantage of you either. However, always keep a certain level of respect between you and your client. When you are an entrepreneur, your clients are all you have so treat them with respect. The type of people you attract and the size of your clientele says a lot about you as an entrepreneur. Be a valuable asset to your clients. Realize you need them beyond money. They bring creativity and purpose. Your clients make you who you are. They help shape and mold the industry culture. Both parties are very valuable to one another. Every once in a while, have a customer appreciation day. Let customers know they are appreciated.

A TITLE DOES NOT MAKE YOU A LEADER

Ownership is just a title, but leadership is more impactful. Being a leader is a unique skill. Not everyone possesses those qualities. Having the money and resources to open an establishment is great. However, real leadership qualities have to be in you and developed over time.

A leader knows how to get the best out of people. A leader will make a person look at themselves in the mirror and try to figure out what they could do better. A true leader leads by example. He or she does not ask you to do something they are not doing themselves. Leaders have a proven track record for success beyond money. It's about being an inspiration to all.

Being a leader has its hurdles. Just because people in your room or inner circle don't follow your lead does not mean you're an ineffective leader. Sometimes your leadership can be felt in rooms you're not in. Your impact can stretch far even when not easily apparent. Never give up on your influence.

No matter the field, leaders will face some form of opposition. Jealously will make people attack the flaws of leaders. Keep in mind, some people will try to undermine leaders. Normally, it stems from their issues with authority. A leader's job is to get the best out of each individual. However, if someone on your team does not want the best for themselves they will definitely not want to listen to you. Being a leader is tricky. Overtime, develop an authentic leadership style that works best for you.

DON'T BLOCK EVERY CLIENT

You will never have the perfect client base. If you can get 90% of your clients to conform to how you do business, you are doing good. Especially if you have a large client base. When you are in a client-driven business, sometimes people are going to be late or people are going to miss appointments. Just because they miss a few appointments or are late a few times does not mean you cut them off. Instead, charge them a late fee (inconvenience fee).

Now, if you have someone who is habitually late or missing appointments, have a conversation with that individual about respecting your time. Let them know your time is valuable and those slots can be used by clients who are serious about coming. Clients need warnings before you cut them off. If they really don't respect your schedule, you can advise them to come in as a walk-in and let anyone service them. You have to meet people where they are. If they are too busy for appointments, being a walk-in may be best for them.

Too many times, small business entrepreneurs cut clients off before exploring all options. You may need the client on the back end. Deal with them accordingly. However, blocking someone after a one-time offense is unnecessary. If it's a first-time client, it's best to call or text them an hour or two before their service begins to ensure they are coming. If one of your regulars is late or misses an appointment, give them a consultation about it on their next scheduled service. As an independent contractor, you have the night to reuse service, but let that be your last resort. Unless someone disrespects you purposefully, do your job and keep it moving.

GIVE YOUR CLIENTS A PROPER CONSULT

There are too many forms of communication for your clients to be confused about scheduling, pricing, and the service they're booking. Miscommunication and confusion will cause you to lose existing clients and potential clients. All of your services should be listed online and in your business brochure. Consider your website as a menu of offerings. Clients should be able to navigate through your website (menu) with ease.

One thing clients don't want is to feel tricked or nickeled and dimed so avoid hidden fees! Nobody wants to sign up for one service, then get charged a different price after the service. If a client signs up for the wrong service, explain that to them before you start. Have all clients, especially new clients, arrive at least fifteen minutes early to discuss or prep for service. When you only offer limited services on your booking site, it requires you to provide detailed explanations in person.

Another consideration is type or tier of service. When you only offer a deluxe service, it limits you being a consideration for certain clients. As an entrepreneur, it's not your job to appease every person's budget, but it is your job to explain the options thoroughly and deliver—every time. Sometimes clients want a basic service. If your basic service comes with a premium price tag, that's fine, but be prepared to answer questions.

If you sell products or merchandise, those should be included on your website as well. Clients should know the benefit of each product and how it could enhance their everyday needs. If done properly, your business will grow expeditiously. Lastly, don't let clients dictate your price. If you give a proper consultation and they come in the door bargaining, that's not the ideal client for you. That person wants the best for less. You be the judge of whether you want to give a discount or not.

DON'T DO THE MOST TO GET THE MOST

You don't have to do the most to get the most. When it's time to increase your prices, you will know. But make sure your skills match the price. Don't rush the learning curve or feel the need to succumb to the pressures of what your peers are doing to get money. Do what you need to do for yourself.

When you are doing business, customers can feel when you are rushing them, not interested, or not putting in the best effort. Thus, you have no right to expect premium pay while offering subpar work. Even if you can command higher prices, don't stop giving your best. Continue to work hard at your craft. Be committed. The people are the ones who are going to tell you your worth. You'll know by your demand. When your demand is high it means you're doing the right things. People trust you to be consistent, reliable, and knowledgeable.

IT TAKES MONEY TO MAKE MONEY

Everyone knows it takes money to make money. It's called an investment. In order for a business to get off the ground, it requires startup funds and if you don't have capital or business credit, it can be tough.

If you know what you want to do, start planning early by saving or thinking through a financial plan. A good practice is putting a specific amount aside every week. Try to cut out unnecessary outings and expenses. Concurrently, build a relationship with a business banker so you can get expert guidance and support. A business banker will evaluate your personal credit, business credit, and additional tradelines that you may need. Also try to gather prices for your equipment early by getting at least three quotes. Write down a detailed list of business needs so you can start to create your budget. Everything costs money. Nothing, or nearly nothing, will be free. So, start planning early then go get it!

DON'T CHASE THE CELEBRITY

Make your clients look like celebrities, don't chase celebrities. Celebrity clients will come to you based on word of mouth and you outperforming. However, running behind celebrities to boost clientele is some groupie shit. Typically, when you try to specifically seek them out, they don't respect you. Let them come to you based on your talent. Don't get lost in the sauce.

If you build a business based solely on celebrities and your relationship with the celebrity/celebrities goes left, you have to start over. There are more non-celebrities than celebrities so think about that. It's simple math. Keep your day-to-day customers. Sometimes the extra few dollars from a celebrity isn't enough for the trouble of having to move your schedule around to accommodate them. Put celebrities on your schedule like everyone else. Have them come to your business to support you there. However, running all over the city to chase down one individual is a waste of time. Treat everyone the same way. Only step outside your routine if it's beneficial to you. Don't get caught up in the hype of who a person is versus what a person is actually doing for you. Remember, celebrities need your services just as much as the next person. If you operate at a high level, keep doing that. Keep making your demand strong and the right people will request you.

SHOP TALK: ETHICS

Don't come in the shop saying any ol' thing just to have something to say. Eyes and ears are watching and listening and your words can send the wrong message.

People shop at local businesses for service, entertainment, news, and the latest gossip. It's part of the industry and culture. However, you want to be as accurate with the information shared as possible. Sometimes at shops, all types of lies get told, from clients and barbers alike. People sometimes just want to put on a show. However, everyone may not be into the foolishness. Keep in mind, just because you like playing around, everyone else may not be on the same thing you're on. Find a way to be neutral when you can. You don't always have to comment or add a perspective.

The shop is definitely a place where people gather to share information. Just don't be ignorant with it. Young kids frequent barber shops, too. Be mindful of who is in your chair and close by. Having fun is cool but always keep it professional. Whenever you operate unprofessionally, you leave the door open for anything to happen. The shop may feel like a hangout spot, but it's a business first. When you conduct business, your approach to everything must be intentional. But if you start treating your business as though everything goes, so will clients. Shop talk is cool, but always operate with tact. Keep it business and you will succeed.

CAN'T TEACH EFFORT

You can teach technique, but you can't teach effort. Effort to grow, learn, and evolve all come from within. The old adage is you can take a horse to the well, but you can't make him drink. If you don't want to grow, you will be in the same spot mentally, financially, and maybe worse, physically. Life is about evolving because everything changes with time. What you do with that time is very important. Doing the bare minimum will never get you ahead. The new wave is getting rich quick. However, that's a false reality. If you want more out of life, you have to grind for it. Anybody who owns a business or became a CEO of a company, put in the adequate time and effort to be where they are today. The longer you put effort into something, the better the results will be. If you spend your free time playing around on social media or anything unproductive, you will never be successful. We are all where we are in life due to specific choices and decisions we've made. If you're in a hole, dig yourself out of it. Barriers and road blocks will always exist but at the end of any day, we all got the same 24 hours. What you do with your time is on you. Will you focus on grinding and hustling to advance yourself? It's your call.

MASTER ONE THING FIRST

If you have a gift, operate in your gift. Don't try to muddy the waters by spreading yourself across several things before you master one of your gifts.

If you own a business, you want people to have a clear idea of who you are and what you do instantly. They should be able to link you with your primary source of income—that business. There's nothing wrong with having multiple streams of income, but let them branch off the main source. They should be connected and somewhat related or you need to keep them completely independent.

If you open a barbershop, a t-shirt line and hair product line can align with that. However, if you have different streams of income not affiliated with your primary source, it can be complicated and confusing for clients and potential clients. It even becomes confusing for your communication and marketing efforts. When you open several businesses, it takes time to develop them. To be successful in all of the businesses, you have to strategic in your choices. Haphazardly starting new income streams doesn't benefit you in the long-term and can cannibalize your main source of income. To be clear, there is nothing wrong with being ambitious, but also be calculated. Make your next move a smart move.

INCREASE YOUR VALUE

There's a difference between price and value. The price is what people pay, the value is what they get out of it. Prices are set by the seller and therefore, arbitrary. Value is determined by the buyer and can be different for every person. If the value of your service is clear for people, they will pay the price you set. Whenever you do something rare, you create more value for yourself.

Don't be so focused on increasing your price that you lose sight of the value being created. Even in your marketing and communications, emphasize value, not prices. Some of the largest retailers you know have volume strategies that focus on price. They are low cost leaders. They want more people to buy and therefore, keep their prices low and their costs even lower to guarantee a profit. But there are others that are value-driven and therefore, they have premium pricing to match. Because they know what they deliver to customers and it extends before the cash amount. What is your strategy—volume or value?

If your use the volume method, your prices will be lower and your rotation time should be faster to turn a profit. Over time, if you're reliable, efficient, and skilled, you will be able to make a lot of money because you'll have the volume. If you go with the value method, you will likely have a slower rotation with less customers overall but the clients you do have will pay a premium price. Over time, you can still make just as much or more than a volume-based business.

THE ROOT, THE START, THE BEGINNING

B efore becoming entrepreneurs, we were all amateurs. That's where the organic love, passion, and enjoyment began. As amateurs, it was about so much more than money. However, entrepreneurship was when we turned our passion into a paycheck.

Some careers begin as hobbies for people and they eventually create businesses from them. Think about cooking, barbering, braiding, personal training, auto mechanic, etc. But for many in these professions, they went to school, trained, and became certified. They took it seriously and sought the expertise needed to treat it like more than a hobby. It does not mean you can't become great at the trade, but it may take you more time to develop and reach expert status.

Sometimes, things don't work out and, in those moments, don't stay in an industry messing up the reputation for everyone else because you can't do it. If you try to force something that wasn't meant for you, you're going to be miserable. Choose a career that brings you joy.

UNPLUG

You have to know when to unplug. As entrepreneurs, we go so hard for what we're building, it's hard to turn the intensity off. However, you have to learn how to unplug to be able to give some of that same energy to your family and loved ones. The people who support you and know you best deserve some of your time. On your down time, go visit them or give them a call. Check on people to let them know you still care.

The relationships you had before you became an entrepreneur were essential in molding who you are today. When you unplug, get some rest because it is always needed. Without rest, your mind can ultimately become fatigued. When you unplug, don't let phone calls about the business consume you unless it's one you have to take. Other than that, put your phone down. When you unplug, try at least one new activity because it keeps your mind fresh. Sometimes new activities give you a new life. You may find a new hobby while partaking in that activity. When you unplug, read a book. There are many things you can learn when you decide to read. Reading keeps the mind sharp. Unplugging is essentially about getting your mind right. So many times, business owners and entrepreneurs take their work home with them. They're doing things before and after work for the business. Being an entrepreneur is definitely not easy, but try to enjoy the fruits of your labor.

PHOTOGRAPHY

We are in a visual society and people buy what they see. Your pictures give validation to your talents, vision, artistic ability, industry, and culture. When you put out different images, you want them to be clear and concise. Don't just post anything because everything reflects you. The angles, lighting, and tone of a picture are important to your delivery. Your audience will build their perception of your business based on what you post. Put your best foot forward.

Once you can afford it, invest in a professional camera and a ring light to help get better lighting in your photos. Between the camera and ring light, this will enhance the quality of work that you post to your business accounts. Also record and post quick videos. People love to see you market yourself with the business. You can also run a sponsored ad through any social media outlet to gain more followers. If people see your pictures, videos, and content looking great, they are going to be intrigued to give you a try.

CAREER VISIONING

Career visioning is about building a team by attracting and hiring talent. The success of your brand will be determined more by the people you partner and build with rather than the number of customers you serve. You have to think bigger.

If your goal requires more than your personal energy allows, you need a team. You need others to help achieve your goals. When you have a big vision, others can buy into it and help you make it grow. It's a win-win. But make sure you go deep—build trusting connections of value. Quality is better than quantity. Who you get into a relationship with in business reflects your brand, business, and culture. You are the sum of the five closest people to you so pick them carefully. If your business is not operating at the level you want, it may be because of who you let in. Sometimes, you have to clean house and start all over. Career visioning is about where you see your business in the future and the steps it will take to get there. To make progress, you must first have a vision and set goals and then execute.

MONEY TALKS

In life, people are going to talk a lot. Some say this. Some say that. However, at the end of the day, money talks. A true entrepreneur and business man makes deals. It takes money and resources to close these deals. When networking, connect with the people who are really doin' it big. Those are the people with real insight. People who really doing great things, don't mind sharing information with those who are humble and got some hustle about themselves. The sad reality is broke minded people can't really do anything for you but bring you down. Broke minded people typically have now money and no resources. If you want to level up in life and in your career, you have to associate with the people who are making the moves. You can still stay true to your core values, but you can expand your horizon by associating with the leaders. Once you are in the right circle, you begin to think differently, move differently, act accordingly. All change isn't bad. Change is good when it's for the betterment of your life. In order to grow, the have to cut loose of old chains that were holding you back. Get around likeminded individuals who can help you succeed. Sometimes what was real to you twenty years prior ain't real no more. Life is about progressing. When good information is being spilled, take heed to it. You may learn something that can take you a long way.

PARTNERSHIP VS. SOLE PROPRIETORSHIP

A partnership is an arrangement where parties, known as business partners, agree to cooperate to advance their mutual interests. The partners in a partnership may be individuals, businesses, interest-based organizations, schools, governments, or combinations. Organizations may partner to increase the likelihood of each achieving their mission and to amplify their reach. A partnership may result in issuing and holding equity or may be only governed by a contract.

A sole proprietorship, also known as the sole trader, individual entrepreneurship or proprietorship, is a type of enterprise that is owned and ran by one person and in which there is not legal distinction between the owner and business entity. A sole trader does not necessarily work alone. It's possible for the sole trader to employ other people. The sole trader receives all profits and has unlimited responsibility for all losses and debts.

Partnerships can be beneficial depending on the situation. However, doing a partnership on a booth rental shop/physical location can be tricky. In a partnership, every decision is made with another person. It can be tougher if one person works at the physical location and the other person just collects money. In a partnership, everyone must play a role. If you partner with someone who does not know the business, it could possibly lead to friction between both parties. A partnership could work well if all parties involved are doing what they need to do for the business to grow. There's a big difference between operating a business and handling outside business affairs. You need both in order for a business to thrive.

If you operate as a sole proprietor, all aspects of the business depend on you. You will be responsible for rent, payroll, human resources, marketing, and all overhead that comes with it. However, there's a bigger reward for owning by yourself. You make your own decisions, hire and fire who you want, and expand as needed. The best part about being a sole proprietor is all revenue comes back to you and you don't have to report to anybody. There is more work to do but less to think about when you make your decisions.

NEVER GIVE ANOTHER BUSINESS PERSON ALL YOUR MONEY UNTIL THE PROJECT IS DONE

When entering into a business deal with a company or freelancer, don't pay everything upfront. Pay half or pay a deposit. If you pay the entire invoice and the work is incomplete or not to your liking, you are at a disadvantage and have no leverage. Unfortunately, everyone does not do business the right way. Once that other business or freelancer receives full payment, that's likely it. Instead, give the person something to work for. Keep them accountable. Sometimes, people get their money and disappear without finishing the job or the work quality is rushed. Set guidelines and timeframes and if the project is not completed at maximum quality, don't pay the full price until it's done right. You should feel good about the outcome without being jerked around during the process. A good business relationship operates in good faith and quality work.

KEEP GOING!!!

Nothing good comes from comfort zones. You have to continue to apply pressure. When you keep going, you will be able to look back on how far you have come. When you stay stagnant, you won't accomplish anything. The world is going to continue to grow. However, if you don't move with the times, you will be left behind.

The most successful people in life weren't always the smartest, but they had enough common sense to keep going. When things get tough, you have to dig deep and find a way through. Quitters never win and winners never stop. To make it to the top of the food chain, you have to put in weeks, months, and years of grind. If you want your situation to change, you have to keep going! You have to run on and see what the end will be.

If you face rejection of some sort, that's okay. Rejection is protection. God has something better in store for you. If you stop after one roadblock, you will never reach your destiny. Get up out of your bed. Put your phone down. Leave your comfort zone. Push forward. Michael Jordan didn't become arguably the greatest basketball player by making one shot. He put hours upon hours into his craft. Keep going until what you dream comes to fruition.

STAY AWAY FROM NEGATIVE-MINDED PEOPLE

Negative-minded people can't do anything but pull you down. Most negative-minded people don't believe in themselves so they try to inject that fear onto others. When you notice that type of behavior, move away from the person quickly. A person with negative energy will try to diminish your dreams and aspirations. Link up with those who will inspire you and uplift you. A positive-minded person sees the good in everything even during tough times. A negative-minded person only sees negativity in most things and due to their own limiting beliefs, chose not to pursue their goals in life. One who is negative-minded is too fearful of rejection or they failed at something they tried before and can't figure out how to move past their own insecurity. Just because someone before you failed at something does not mean that has to be you. A negative-minded person normally shifts the energy in the room. If a person always has bad vibes or something negative to say, they are probably dealing with something internally and they need help. In the meantime, don't waste your time trying to fix them. If you can encourage them, of course you should do so. However, don't waste all your energy trying to fix someone else's issues. If someone wants to run in place, let them have that, but don't stick around. Align yourself with positivity.

YOUR BUSINESS EIN

Are we doing business or are we doing business? So many self-proclaimed entrepreneurs are doing business without the proper business acumen. In order for your business to be legitimate, you will need a few things. If you don't get your business creditability together, you will always be operating "under the table" in the business world.

Operating under the table is not good long term because everything you buy will have to be placed under someone else's name. In order to operate a business, you have to first understand business. The Employer Identification Number (EIN) also known as the Federal Employer Identification Number (FEIN) or the Federal Tax Identification Number, is a unique nine-digit number assigned by the Internal Revenue Service (IRS) to business entities operating in the United States for the purposes of identification. Your EIN is basically your business social security number. Your business is required to have this number for three main purposes:

1. To identify your business and make sure you are accountable for your actions
2. To protect the public health and safety
3. To keep track of your finances for tax purposes

Business licenses are authorized to operate in a geographic area, most commonly the county or city where you are based.

BOOKKEEPING

Bookkeeping is the recording of financial transactions and is part of the process of accounting in business, sales receipts, and payments by an individual person on an organization/corporation. There are several standard methods of bookkeeping including the single-entry and double entry bookkeeping systems. While these may be viewed as "real" bookkeeping, my process for recording financial transactions is a bookkeeping process. It is important for entrepreneurs to write everything down. Bookkeeping allows you to keep your finances in order so you know how much you are making and spending. A proper system allows you to track and manage in one place.

A simple and free solution is a spreadsheet. You can also invest in bookkeeping software or hire a CPA or bookkeeping company. Whatever the method, find a way to stay on top of the money you bring in and the money going out of your business daily.

PURPOSE-DRIVEN

Find your purpose and stay there. Find what makes you happy to get up in the morning. Find what it is that drives you to be the best version of yourself and inspire others. When you are living in your purpose, you will be the happiest you've ever been. When you are operating in your purpose, other people can feel that energy. When you know what your purpose is, you can start making a difference in your life and the life of others. However, when you are not living in your purpose, you will become angry, miserable, and annoyed at just about anything. When you are not operating in your purpose, you will probably not even want to be at work, home, school, or whatever it is that you're doing.

You must find what makes you happy. Someone who is purpose-driven makes intentional and strategic moves. When you live a purpose-driven life, you have a vision and goal for yourself. Purpose-driven people create clarity in their engagement, motives, and efforts. Find what it is that will help you complete your mission, vision, and objectives. If not, you're just wasting your most valuable resource—time.

SUPPORT YOUR OWN

We must give back and support our communities. If we do not support our own, we as a people won't last. You can do something as simple as reposting a friend's business page. There are so many things we can do from sending donations, buying products, booking appointments, reposting work, etc.

There is strength in numbers. We all need each other equally. If we work together, we can be unstoppable. Working together helps ensure more locations, more endorsements, more exposure, and more business. We need our communities to grow and everyone has to do their part. Major corporations aren't giving us the support we need so we need our people to pull together so we can create and build from within. Support your own and be glad to do it the right way. We as a people don't want to look back and see our favorite businesses no longer around. We have the ability to change that trajectory. Black-owned businesses can't survive off hugs, handshakes, and discounts. We *must* stimulate our own economy first.

TAKE EMOTIONS OUT OF BUSINESS DECISIONS

Business is business. Owning and leading are tough and it takes a certain type of person to stay constant and disciplined enough to remain in business. One of the key principles to longevity is to remove emotion.

When you are doing what you love, it's going to be hard to separate the emotions that naturally come with it. However, you have to make sure you keep everything business first. Unless someone totally disrespects you, don't take their words or actions personally. Sometimes it's best to take a breath and step back before you make any major decisions. Sometimes you may need to write out the pros and cons before you act. Sometimes you may have to sleep on a decision before you make it. Either way, don't let your emotions lead you.

PRACTICAL TASKS + TIPS

- Prepare and practice your elevator pitch so you know what your business is about and who your business is for and how your business impacts the world. Ask friends if they'll give you feedback as to what they would think about you if they didn't know you and heard you say it. Go back and adjust as needed and as your situation changes.

- Go out and meet five new people every day. Be sure to pitch with passion. It's not only what you say that makes a difference, but how you say it. Deliver your introduction with energy and enthusiasm.

- Enroll in free communication courses.

- Continue to learn about your style, what works, where you get stuck, and ways you can complement your natural strengths with new behaviors. You can do this by asking for feedback from seasoned professionals in the industry. Gain a deeper understanding of the industry by becoming a student of the industry, following those who are doing well, and focusing on developing and mastering your skills.

- Remember, your prices should reflect your versatility and experience. You should know the difference between competitive prices and premium prices.

- Make a price list chart explaining all products and services so your clients will not be surprised when they come to your chair. Your price chart and products should be visible on your website. In addition, your cuts and hairstyles should be visible in order to show proof of your work.

- At the beginning of each day, define what you want to accomplish. This is considered making small goals to crush every day.

- Every morning before you walk into the workplace, say a prayer before you start your day and mediate on positive thoughts. This will allow your mind and spirit to stay humble and work hard throughout your day.

- Never forget how you started in this industry and the people who assisted your growth and maturity. Show gratitude and humility.

- Remember, clients do not have to give you their business. Therefore, you should be appreciative of every client who comes to your chair. When you finish, always say, "Thank you for your service."

- If you find it hard to be humble, set a timer for every hour. Once that hour occurs, take a few seconds to think about your ego during that hour. If it needs to be adjusted, ryou always have the next client to get it right. If you feel that you conducted yourself in a humble matter within that hour, think on ways of how you can do even better than before.

- Identify a few people you admire and ask if they would be willing to spend thirty minutes to one hour a month or even a quarter with you answering questions about the industry. Be specific about the amount of time you are asking for so they don't think it is going to take an inordinate amount of time. Also, make it clear that you will be responsible for getting on their calendar and for driving the topic.

- Consciously expand your world of possibilities by enumerating your choice at every fork in the road. If you can't see them, brainstorm with your mentor.

- Strive for greatness and read biographies of successful professionals in the industry and learn how they broadened their possibilities.

- Ignore naysayers, understand that greatness has to be inside of you for you to push forward, and know that mediocracy is unacceptable. Challenge yourself each day by finding something to do, and then ask yourself, "Can I do it quicker, faster, stronger, and still be efficient?" With that said, always think outside of the box.

- Most successful people have a coach. It is important to know that successful people do not succeed by themselves.

- Take the best in the industry out to lunch. This way you can pick their brain to understand the task they completed to become successful. Once you understand what they have done, study their work.

- Continue to educate yourself. Learn how to create your own promotional videos and incorporate your own professional photos within the videos.

- Creativity is crucial in this industry. Buy a sketch pad and draw at least once a week so that you can develop different styles for your clients.

- Buy proper attire, make sure your hair is cut, and smell appropriate for your clients.

- Take time to learn new techniques. Don't borrow your co-worker's supplies. Take the time to research the best supplies and tools and purchase those for yourself.

- Understand that vision comes to you not from you. You should always begin with the end in mind.

- In order for you to overcome fear, you first need to understand what you are fearful of and embrace and name it. Say it out loud and write it down. Embracing and naming your fear gives you strength to deal with it.

- Once you have embraced your fears, be deliberate, create an action plan, and pace yourself into overcoming the fear.

- Visualize yourself as unafraid of the thing you wrote down. When you visualize yourself being confident and competent about your fears, the image will be accepted in your subconscious mind.

- Continue to move toward your fear. When you continue to move toward your fear, it grows smaller and more manageable to maintain.

- In any industry, foot traffic is important. Foot traffic is people steadily walking about. For instance, being located in a plaza is key.

- A great business model in a bad location is pointless unless you hire people who have their own clientele.

- Post compelling and quality content on your social media. Whatever you decide to share about yourself and your business needs to be engaging and optimized for search engines.

- Choose your connections wisely and manage your privacy settings so your followers can find you.

- Research online for the social media platforms best suited for your followers. You should understand how they use your data, and the conventions that govern the way the community operates before you create your accounts. Once you understand this, pay for social media ads to engage with a broader audience.

- It is important to know your target audience and your target market. Your target market is a specific, well-defined segment of consumers that you plan to target with your products, services, and marketing activities. Target audience is narrower. It refers specifically to the group of consumers targeted by advertisements. For example, if I have a hair and beauty supply company for women, my target market is women and girls of all ages. If I run an advertisement regarding hair bow specials, my target audience will be women between the ages of 25-45 who have young daughters.

- Create a schedule for social media. Know exactly when your followers are online and post your content to ensure they will engage.

- Create a business page. This way you can control your personal information. It is not good to have your business page and your personal page as one profile.

- Acknowledge and appreciate your connections. Share their posts and endorse/recommend them when possible.

- Continue to learn your style, what works, where you get stuck, and ways you can complement your natural strengths with behaviors that you have to adapt to within your work environment.

- Be conscious of the fact that behavioral expectations vary among people and cultures. What works for one co-worker may not work for another.

- Always examine your mind. Don't surround yourself with people who drain your aspiration, who are negative and don't want to build you up. Surround yourself with people who are positive, who will build you up, and who will nurture positive beliefs within you.

- Each day, take small steps. Accomplishing a small goal every day makes you feel better and builds your faith in yourself. Challenge yourself to a task that you have never tried before so that you can keep mind moving forward at all times. Also, your mind will not be static.

- Pay attention to your mindset and what you are thinking about each day. If you are putting yourself down, reverse those thoughts and try focusing on your positive traits. Remember, what you think about yourself influences the results you're getting in everyday life.

- Be willing to go against societal norms.

- Stay enthusiastic. Know that failure is part of a growth mindset. Fail fast and cheaply. Do a post-analysis of each failure.

- Develop competence. Your competency is your confidence.

- Every morning before you wake up take deep breathes to allow your mind to focus on the day that is to come. Prayer and meditation are vital in order to get your mind positive at all times.

- Do not focus on negative thoughts any more than you absolutely have to. Don't give it energy.

- You must keep the end result in mind and fight temptation. Research has proven that our environment affects our choices. Therefore, if the environment or the company you deal with daily affects your choice, it is time for you to remove yourself from that situation.

- You must know your weaknesses and stay away from activities that will take you off track.

- Stop trying to do everything yourself. Build a team of professionals to help you with every aspect of your business.

- When setting goals, you must connect with your vision. This is the thing that pulls you forward, inspires, and excites you. Think about how your business will look within the next three years. You also want to write down your vision in order to connect it with your goals. Make your goals S.M.A.R.T. Make sure your goals are specific, measurable, actionable, realistic and time-framed.

- To set long-term goals, draw a picture of where you see yourself within ten years. Ask yourself why? Why are you setting the goal? Is it to make more money? Is it to ensure you have a flexible lifestyle? Is it to start a family? Take time to think about your why.

- Avoid circumstances that will trigger unwanted emotions. If there is a client who you know will trigger negative emotions, it would be in your best interest to allow someone in your establishment to cut their hair. Keeping your emotions in tactic is more important than receiving a few dollars for a cut.

- Shift your attentional focus. You may constantly feel inferior to people who are in your environment. Your coworkers may have clients booked back to back, seven days a week, and you may only have five clients per day. Shift your focus to making sure that your five clients' cuts are exceptional. This way, you are focusing on what you're doing, and in the process, you'll gain more clientele.

- Hustle…*hard!*